ROBERT D. BEZUCHA
PROJECT DIRECTOR

NORMAN F. GUESS
EDITORIAL DIRECTOR

R. JAMES ERTEL
MANAGING EDITOR

ALICE F. MARTIN
ASSOCIATE EDITOR

**GENEVIEVE CURLEY
JOAN FALK**

PAULINE NORTON
ASSISTANT PROJECT DIRECTOR

**RICHARD D. HARKINS
HESTER GELB**

CONTRIBUTORS AND CONSULTANTS

Hall Bartlett, Ed.D., Citizenship Education Project, Teachers College, Columbia University; Author

Walt Disney, Motion Picture and Television Producer

Evelyn Millis Duvall, Ph.D., Author and Consultant on Family Life; Authority on Child Development

Edna E. Eisen, Ph.D., Professor of Geography, Kent State University

J. Allen Hynek, Ph.D., Associate Director, Smithsonian Astrophysical Observatory

Leland B. Jacobs, Ph.D., Professor of Education, Teachers College, Columbia University

Eleanor M. Johnson, M.A., Director of Elementary School Services, Graduate Division, Wesleyan University

Herbert A. Landry, M.S., Ph.D., Director, Bureau of Educational Program Research and Statistics, New York City Public Schools

Milton Levine, M.D., Associate Professor of Pediatrics, New York Hospital

Willy Ley, Professor of Science, Fairleigh Dickinson University; Rocket Expert and Author

Norman Lloyd, M.A., Teacher of Literature and Materials of Music, Juilliard School of Music

Lenox R. Lohr, M.E., D.Eng., D.Sc., President, Museum of Science and Industry, Chicago

Will C. McKern, D.S., Former Director, Milwaukee Public Museum; Anthropologist

Richard A. Martin, B.S., Curator, N. W. Harris Public School Extension, Chicago Natural History Museum

Maurice Pate, Executive Director, United Nations Children's Fund (UNICEF)

Norman Vincent Peale, D.D., LL.D., Litt.D., LH.D.; Minister, Marble Collegiate Church, New York; Author

Rutherford Platt, B.A., Member of Two North Pole Expeditions with Admiral MacMillan; Author of Nature Books

Illa Podendorf, M.S., Teacher of Science, University of Chicago Laboratory Schools; Author of Science Books

Mary M. Reed, Ph.D., Supervisor of Little Golden Books; Formerly of Teachers College, Columbia University

John R. Saunders, M.A., Chairman, Department of Public Instruction, American Museum of Natural History

Glenn T. Seaborg, Ph.D., LL.D., D.Sc., Chancellor and Professor of Chemistry, University of California, Berkeley; Associate Director, University of California Radiation Laboratory; Co-winner of Nobel Prize for Chemistry, 1951

Louis Shores, Ph.D., Dean of the Library School, Florida State University; Author and Authority on Reference Materials

Nila Banton Smith, Ph.B., Ph.D., Professor of Education and Director of The Reading Institute, New York University

Bryan Swan, M.S., Teacher of Physical Science, University of Chicago Laboratory Schools; Author

Samuel Terrien, S.T.M., Th.D., Auburn Professor of the Old Testament, Union Theological Seminary

Jessie Todd, M.A., Formerly of the Art Department, University of Chicago; Art Lecturer; Contributor to Art Magazines

Lloyd B. Urdal, Ph.D.,. Assistant Professor, School of Education, State College of Washington

Jane Werner Watson, B.A., Editor and Author of More Than a Hundred Golden Books

William S. Weichert, M.S., Supervisor of Science, Oakland (Calif.) Public Schools

Paul A. Witty, Ph.D., Professor of Education, Northwestern University; Specialist on Gifted Children

THE
GOLDEN BOOK
ENCYCLOPEDIA

VOLUME XIII—RABBITS TO SIGNALING

In Sixteen Accurate, Fact-filled Volumes Dramatically Illustrated
with More Than 6,000 Color Pictures

THE ONLY ENCYCLOPEDIA FOR YOUNG GRADE-SCHOOL CHILDREN

ACCURATE AND AUTHORITATIVE

ENTERTAININGLY WRITTEN AND ILLUSTRATED TO
MAKE LEARNING AN ADVENTURE

by Bertha Morris Parker

*Formerly of the Laboratory Schools, University of Chicago
Research Associate, Chicago Natural History Museum*

GOLDEN PRESS · NEW YORK

The letter *R* began as the picture of a person's head ( ). The Egyptians used the picture in their hieroglyphic writing. After it was borrowed for the first alphabet its shape changed so that it was easier to write ( ). The Greeks wrote it first in this way ( ) and then this ( ). The Romans changed it to the shape we know.

R stands for several slightly different sounds. And it is pronounced differently in different parts of the English-speaking world. In some regions the letter is silent unless it comes before a vowel.

RABBITS Many other animals would go hungry if it were not for rabbits. Minks, foxes, weasels, and hawks are among the animals that find rabbits good eating.

Rabbits have no weapons for fighting their enemies. But they have long, strong hind legs that let them make big leaps and bounds as they run away. They have big ears that tell them when an enemy is coming close. Their color as a rule helps them hide because it is about the same color as their surroundings. They can stay very still so that they do not give away their hiding place by moving. If they are running away, they can stop suddenly and change direction fast.

One other thing helps rabbits hold their own. They have many babies. A mother cottontail may have several families in a year, and there are from two to six babies in each family. The mother cottontail takes good care of her babies. She lines the nest for them with soft hair she pulls from her own furry coat.

Rabbits themselves eat only plants. Wild rabbits often eat carrots and cabbages in gardens. Rabbits have good teeth for gnawing and can make quick work of a carrot.

There are several breeds of tame rabbits. Their ancestor was not the American cottontail but the wild rabbit found in Europe. Rabbits were first tamed in Europe. People raised them for food. In America they were first raised as pets. Now they are raised not only for pets but also for their meat and their fur. The pet rabbits most often seen are white and have pink eyes. They are albinos.

The jack rabbit of the American West, although it is a very close relative of the

Snowshoe Rabbit (Winter)

WILD RABBITS

Desert Cottontail

Snowshoe Rabbit (Summer)

DOMESTICATED RABBITS

Belgian Hare

Himalayan Rabbit

rabbit, is not a rabbit. Neither is the snow-shoe rabbit. Both are actually hares. Just as some hares are called rabbits, some true rabbits are called hares. The Belgian hare is a rabbit. True rabbits are born naked and blind. Hares are born with fur and with their eyes open. (See ALBINO; FURS; PETS; PROTECTIVE COLORING.)

RACES OF MANKIND Scientists call every different kind of animal in the world a species. The yellow-headed blackbird, for instance, is one species. The red-winged blackbird is another. The rusty blackbird is still another. Scientists give every species a scientific name. It is a Latin name, and in many cases it is long and hard to pronounce. The scientific name of the yellow-headed blackbird is *Xanthocephalus xanthocephalus*. The scientific name of the red-winged blackbird is *Agelaius phoenicius*. The scientific name of the rusty blackbird is *Euphagus carolinus*.

All the people in the world belong to the same species. An American Indian looks very different from a fair-haired native of Sweden. A Hottentot looks very different from an Eskimo. But they are all really much alike. Almost all the differences are in outward appearance. Every single person in the world belongs to the species scientists call *Homo sapiens*.

Although all people are very much alike in the way they are built, some are more alike than others. An American Indian is more like an Eskimo than he is like an African Pygmy. An Arab is more like a native of India than like a Chinese. Scientists have used likenesses and differences to divide all the earth's people into races.

In dividing people into races scientists have used shape of head, height, color of skin, color of eyes, color of hair, form of hair, cheekbones, shape of nose, shape of mouth, and other such things.

Some races are more alike than others. There are three big groups. They are commonly called white, black, and yellow.

MONGOLOID

Chinese

Sinic (China and Japan)
Mongol (Central Asia)
American Indian (America)
Eskimo (America)

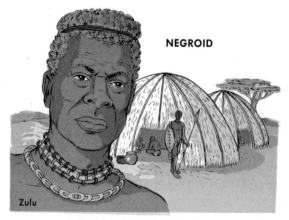

NEGROID

Zulu

True Negro (Western Africa)
Bantu (Southern Africa)
Bushman-Hottentot (Southern Africa)
Melanesian (Pacific Islands)

CAUCASOID

Norwegian

Nordic (Northwestern Europe)
Alpine (Central Europe)
Mediterranean (Southern Europe)
Indo-Dravidic (India)
Arabic (Asia Minor)

These names are based on skin color. But they are not very good names. For some races in the white group have dark-brown skins. Some of the races in the black group have light-brown skins. And some of those in the yellow group have skins that are reddish-brown. The scientific names given to these groups are "Caucasoid," "Negroid," and "Mongoloid."

The captions under the illustrations name some of the races in each group. Many people do not know to what race they themselves belong. If, for instance, the fair-haired man in the picture were asked to what race he belonged, he would probably say "white." But he belongs to *one* of the white races. He is a Nordic.

In the list of races there are no such names as German, Brazilian, Swedish, or Canadian. Such names tell to what nation a person belongs. It does not tell anything at all about his race. George Washington and Booker T. Washington were both famous Americans, but they belonged to different races.

Some people get races and religions confused. Some think, for instance, that the Moslems are a race. Instead they are followers of the religion called Islam. Almost all members of the Arab race are Moslems, but some are not, and there are many Moslems who are not Arabs.

When Hitler was the ruler of Germany, he said that he wanted his country to be a nation of pure Aryans. It was a very foolish thing for him to say, for "Aryan" is not the name of a race. It is the name of a group of languages and the peoples who speak them. Besides there is today no such thing as a pure race. There has been a great deal of mixing together.

Scientists tell us that no one has any right to boast of his race. They are not able to find that one race is any more capable than any other. The people of one race can do just as well as those of another if they have the same opportunities. (See ANTHROPOLOGY; MAN.)

RADAR Almost everyone has heard echoes. Sound waves strike something solid and are bounced back. In radar, radio waves are echoed. They strike something they cannot go through and are bounced back. When they come back to the place they started from they are made to strike a special screen. It is much like a television screen. The screen shows in a simple way what the waves have hit. Whatever was hit appears as a light "blip." If many waves bounce back from an object, the "blip" is brighter than if only a few waves bounce back from it.

Some surfaces are better to bounce a ball against than others. It is the same with radar waves. The operator has to learn to read the picture on his screen.

Radar waves are very short radio waves. They travel as fast as light—186,000 miles a second — just as all radio waves do. A radar operator gets his picture very quickly. But it does take a tiny part of a second for the waves to travel to an object and back again. Measuring that time helps tell how far away the object is.

At a radar station there must be a transmitter to send out the radio waves. There must also be a receiving set with a screen. There must be, too, a special kind of antenna. With this antenna the radio waves, instead of going out in all directions, are made to go out in a beam like the beam of a searchlight.

In its early days radar was called Radio Detection and Ranging. The name "radar" comes from five letters in that long name. The letters are underlined.

Radar helped save England during World War II. German bombers were doing great damage to English cities. But then radar began to be used to spot enemy planes approaching. Antiaircraft guns and fighting planes could go into action.

Radar helped greatly in other fighting areas, too. Just as it helped to protect cities against air raids it helped bomber pilots find their targets. Even if a city was hidden by smoke and fog, a pilot could locate it by radar. Radar helped warships aim at enemy ships hidden by smoke screens. It helped shore batteries guard against attacks.

Today many nations have radar stations on their borders. They are an important part of defense in this age of air warfare. A line of radar stations far north in North America is called the DEW (Distant Early Warning) line.

But radar is not just for wartime. It has important peacetime uses, too. One of them is to help the weatherman. Drops of rain reflect radar waves. Radar lets the weatherman keep track of hurricanes. Radar helps the pilots of airlines avoid storms. It is very useful at airports. When visibility is poor, it helps planes land safely. The operator in the airport control tower can see on his radar screen just where every plane approaching the airport is. He can give directions for landing to each pilot by radio.

Radar helps seamen bring their ships safely into port. It warns them if there are icebergs in their paths.

Radar waves have actually traveled to the moon and back, a distance of almost half a million miles. Perhaps in time they will let us see through the clouds on Venus and solve some of the mysteries of Mars. (See AIRPLANES; AIRPORTS; ELECTRONICS; RADIO; TELEVISION; WEATHER.)

RADIO For most of us radio means listening to programs. We turn a knob to send a current of electricity flowing through our radio sets. We turn another knob to bring in the special program we want. Perhaps it is a concert coming from across the sea. Perhaps it is a baseball game only a few miles away. We hear each note of the concert as soon as if we were in the concert hall. We know about a home run as soon as it is made on the playing field.

But radio is helpful in other ways besides bringing us programs. Ships use it to find out exactly where they are and to ask for help if they need it. Airplane pilots use it to talk with the man in the control tower. Explorers use it to keep in touch with the world. Police calls are sent to squad cars by radio. Telephone companies use radio in

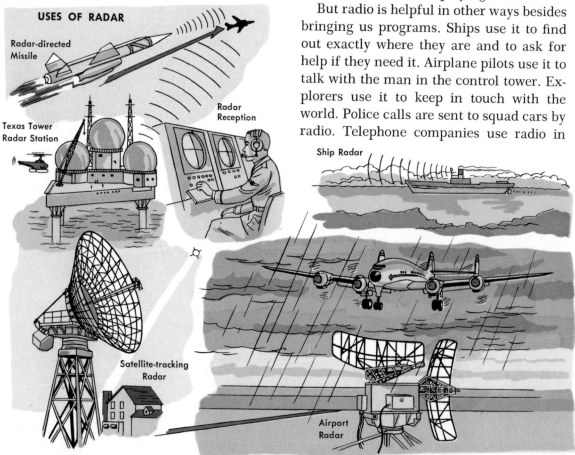

USES OF RADAR

Radar-directed Missile

Texas Tower Radar Station

Radar Reception

Satellite-tracking Radar

Ship Radar

Airport Radar

some cases to carry telephone messages across the ocean.

Some people believe that sound travels all the way from the sending sets to the receiving sets. But this idea is wrong. Only radio waves travel from sending sets to receiving sets. The sound coming from a radio set is made in the set itself. At the sending set sound waves help to produce radio waves. These invisible radio waves travel out into space in all directions. When they reach a receiving set they can be made to produce sound waves exactly like those at the sending station.

No one person can be called the inventor of radio. Many scientists have helped make it into the radio of today. Among the scientists who deserve a great deal of credit for it are the German scientist Heinrich Hertz, the Italian scientist Guglielmo Marconi, and the American scientist Lee De Forest.

Hertz found out that an electric spark sends out waves which can produce another spark a short distance away. By using electric sparks and the waves they send out Marconi found a way of sending messages. This way became known as the wireless telegraph. Messages were sent in a code composed of dots and dashes.

The electron tube called the triode, which was invented by De Forest, was a big step forward in making possible the development of modern radio. Electron tubes are now the heart of our sending sets and most of our receiving sets.

At a broadcasting station special electron tubes in the transmitter produce a carrier signal. This carrier signal is a current that flows back and forth an amazing number of times a second. At the same time the carrier signal is being produced, the sound made in front of a microphone is modifying a current much as a telephone transmitter does. The current is then made stronger, or amplified. This strengthened current, called the audio signal, is sent on wires to the transmitter. There the audio signal is "mixed" with the carrier signal.

USES OF RADIO

Aircraft Traffic Control

Ship-to-shore Radio

ON THE AIR STAND BY

Commercial Broadcasting

Home Reception

Police Radio

The combined audio and carrier signal rushes up and down an aerial unbelievably fast. When a radio announcer says, "This station broadcasts on a frequency of 800 kilocycles," it means that the station's current flows up and down the aerial 800,000 times each second!

The current rushing up and down the aerial sends radio waves out in all directions. These waves travel at the speed of light—186,000 miles a second.

When radio waves hit the antenna of a receiving set, they make a current flow back and forth in it. This current is like the one that flowed up and down the aerial of the sending station, but it is much, much weaker. Three important parts of the receiving set turn this tiny current into sound.

One is the tuner. Waves from many broadcasting stations may be striking the antenna. The tuner lets the listener choose the station he wants to hear.

The current produced by the waves from this one station goes to the detector. It is the job of the detector to change the current into one which can operate the loudspeaker. The detector must separate the carrier signal from the audio signal. The audio signal is then strengthened and sent to the loud-speaker. In the loud-speaker, this current produces sounds just like those made in the broadcasting station.

Some of today's radio sets are AM sets. Some are FM. FM sets can be used only within 100 miles or so of the station broadcasting an FM program. AM sets, if they are good, can get programs or messages from thousands of miles away. The difference is in the kinds of waves the broadcasting station sends out. The big advantage of FM broadcasting is that static does not interfere with it.

In some radio sets tiny transistors are used in place of electron tubes. They are made of crystals of germanium. A transistor set may be pocket-sized.

Radio has done a great deal to make the world seem smaller. We learn about interesting happenings almost as soon as they occur. The first really important radio broadcast in the United States was the report of the presidential election on Nov. 2, 1920. Station KDKA in Pittsburgh broadcast the word that Harding had been elected. Of course, today radio has given way in many places to radio with pictures — television. (See ELECTRONICS; SOUND; TELEVISION; TRANSISTOR.)

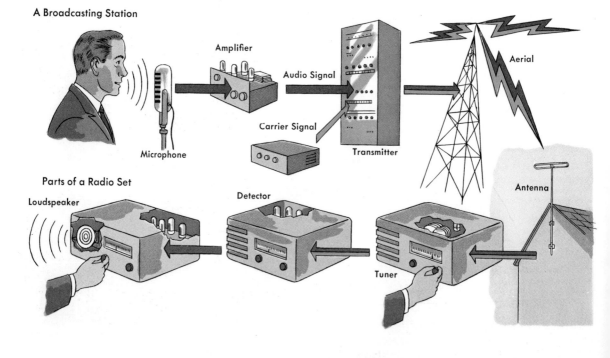

A Broadcasting Station

Amplifier

Audio Signal

Aerial

Carrier Signal

Microphone

Transmitter

Antenna

Parts of a Radio Set

Loudspeaker

Detector

Tuner

RADIUM The early alchemists spent most of their time trying to change common metals such as lead into gold. Many people laughed at the idea. The alchemists had no clear notion of what they were doing. They simply tried all sorts of strange "recipes" and hoped by magic to make the change take place. They wanted to make themselves rich.

Now scientists know that the alchemists were not entirely wrong. For it is possible for certain metals to change into others. The discovery and study of radium showed that this is true. The alchemists would be unhappy, however, because radium, which is thousands of times more expensive than gold, goes through a series of changes and becomes common lead.

Radium is one of the simple substances, or elements, that scientists call radioactive. Radioactive elements change all by themselves into other elements. As they do so, they send out powerful rays. These rays can go through many substances that light cannot go through. The rays from radium, for instance, can go through flesh and be used to treat such diseases as cancer.

A common use of radium is in paint. Paint containing very tiny amounts of this element is used on the hands of clocks and watches to make them glow in the dark. Chemicals in the paint give out flashes of light when hit by rays from the radium.

Carelessly used radium can cause terrible burns. Supplies of it must be kept in special containers with thick lead walls.

Pure radium is a white metal. It is very heavy. But there is so little of it that no one has ever been bothered by its weight. Only a few pounds have been produced in the whole world.

Radium was discovered not much more than half a century ago by the French scientists Pierre and Marie Curie. The story of their work is one of the really exciting chapters in the story of science. (See ALCHEMY; CURIE, MARIE and PIERRE; ELEMENTS; URANIUM.)

RAILROADS May 10, 1869, was an important day in the history of the United States. On that day a spike was driven that joined a railroad being built westward from Omaha, Nebr., with a railroad being built eastward from Sacramento, Calif. The two roads were the Union Pacific and the Central Pacific. They met near Ogden, Utah. For the first time it was possible to travel by railroad all the way across the country.

Railroads now form a great network over the United States. In all, there are more than 350,000 miles — just about enough to reach 15 times around the earth at the equator. The map of the railroads today shows only the more important lines. The country's railroads have had a great deal to do with building it into a strong nation.

Many American cities have grown large partly because they have become great railroad centers. Chicago is the world's greatest railroad center. Hundreds of trains travel in and out of it every day.

It is easy to see how railroads got their name. They are truly roads built of rails. The rails are made of steel and are in sections more than 30 feet long. Heavy spikes fasten them securely to wooden ties from 8 to 9 feet long. The ties are laid on beds of crushed rock, cinders, or gravel. Water can run off easily, and the ties stay firmly in place. A small space is left between one rail and the next when they are laid end

In 1869, the railroads of the East and West met.

Railroad Map of 1860

to end. There must be room for the rails to expand in hot weather. If enough room were not left, a hot day might make the track spread so much that trains would go off it and be wrecked.

The distance of the two rails from each other in a railroad track is called the gauge. Standard gauge is 4 feet, 8½ inches. Most tracks in the United States are built on this gauge. It is possible for cars and engines of one railroad company to run on the tracks of other companies.

Many railroad tracks are double. One track is for trains going in one direction, and the other is for trains going in the other direction. If there is only one track, there must be sidings every so often. A siding is a short track branching away from the main track. When two trains are approaching each other, one of them pulls off on a siding to let the other pass.

Railroad companies build their tracks as nearly level and straight as they can. They avoid sharp corners and steep slopes. If a track must bend, it is laid in a big curve. If a mountain is in the way, the track may wind up and over it, or a tunnel

may be dug through it. Bridges carry tracks over swamps, lakes, and rivers.

Most people probably think of passenger trains when they think of railroads. There are many passenger trains, and they are very important in carrying people from place to place. More than 400 million passengers a year ride on passenger trains in the United States. But carrying freight is an even more important part of the work of most railroads. The freight carried by American railroads amounts to more than a billion *tons* a year. A great deal of our food and many of the other things we use travel at least part of the way to us by freight train.

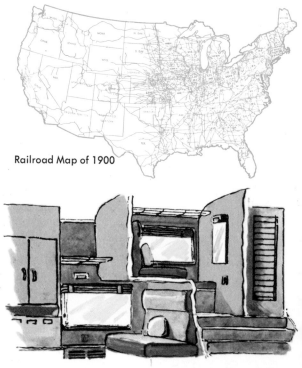

Railroad Map of 1900

Roomettes

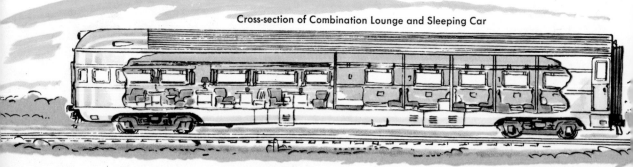

Cross-section of Combination Lounge and Sleeping Car

To carry their passengers and freight, railroads use many kinds of cars. On passenger trains we find coaches, diners, sleepers of several kinds, observation cars, club cars, and baggage cars. Among the many kinds of freight cars are tank cars, flatcars, boxcars, stock cars, refrigerator cars, and coal cars. Some freight now travels "piggyback" on flatcars. Loaded trucks are driven onto these flatcars. They are driven off again at the right city. The freight can then be taken to the exact spot where it is wanted.

Locomotives of different kinds pull the trains. Some are driven by steam. Others are electric or diesel-electric.

With so many trains on the railroads, there must be good signal systems to prevent wrecks. A train crew must know whether the track is clear ahead. They must know when to pull off on a siding. One big danger in stormy weather is that an engineer may not see a signal.

It takes nearly a million people in the United States to keep the country's railroads running. Of course, there are the crews that are on the trains themselves. There are, too, many workers in the railway yards and in the railway stations.

One of the most remarkable things about railroads is how fast they developed. One does not have to go very far back beyond the day the two roads met in Utah to find the very beginning of railroads. Their ancestors were roads of wooden rails over which, in the early 1600's, horses pulled coal cars away from English coal mines. But the modern railroad goes back only to 1825, when the Stockton and Darlington Railway was built in England. The first American railroad built for carrying both freight and passengers was the Baltimore and Ohio. It was started in 1827, but not till several years later did good steam locomotives make regular service satisfactory. How strange a train of those days, with its passenger cars like stagecoaches, would look beside a modern train!

Railroads are not quite so important as they were before the days of automobiles, buses, trucks, and airplanes. But it would still be hard for us to do without them.

Railroad Map of Today

RAIN When water is falling from clouds we say that it is raining. The rain falls in drops. Sometimes the raindrops are small and they fall very gently. A rain of this kind is called a drizzle. Sometimes the rain comes down so fast that no one can see the separate drops. A hard rain of this kind is often called a cloudburst. "Cloudburst" is not really a good name for a heavy rain,

for a cloud cannot burst. There is nothing on the outside of a rain cloud to shut in the drops of water.

Even the smallest drops of rain are much, much larger than the tiny drops of water most clouds are made of. A big raindrop is several million times as big as an ordinary cloud droplet. Cloud droplets may bump into one another and join to form drops big enough to fall. Or, high in a cloud, the droplets may help build up big snowflakes. The big snowflakes then melt as they fall through warm air.

Once in a while it rains when there are no clouds to be seen. What happens is this: There is a cloud several miles above the ground. Rain starts to fall from it. The rain has such a long way to go that the cloud disappears by the time the rain has been able to reach the ground.

Rainfall is measured in inches. If the weatherman says that we have had a one-

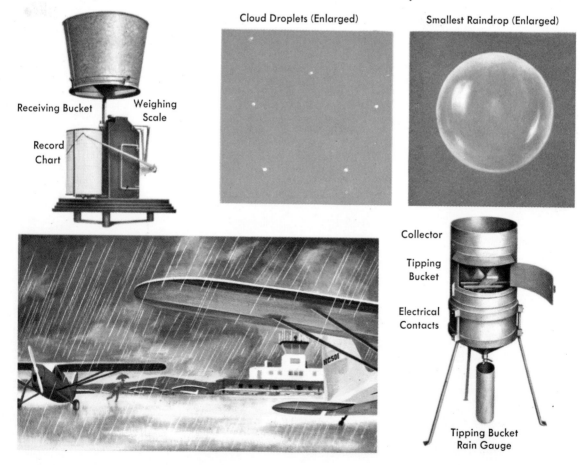

Recording Rain Gauge
(Housing Removed)

Receiving Bucket

Weighing Scale

Record Chart

Cloud Droplets (Enlarged)

Smallest Raindrop (Enlarged)

Collector

Tipping Bucket

Electrical Contacts

Tipping Bucket Rain Gauge

inch rain, he means that enough rain has fallen to make a layer an inch deep on level ground if none sank in. Rain gauges catch rain and measure it. The pictures show two kinds of rain gauges.

A one-inch rain is a heavy rain, but in cloudbursts the rain may be much heavier. The record for one hour was made in Holt, Mo., on June 22, 1947. Twelve inches of rain fell in the hour. The heaviest rainfall for 24 hours was recorded at Baguio in the Philippine Islands in July, 1911. Forty-six inches of rain fell!

In some parts of the world rain is almost unheard of. In Arica, Chile, it takes about 50 years of rainfall to measure an inch. What a contrast with Mt. Waialeali in the Hawaiian Islands, where about 470 inches falls in a year!

There are often clouds when it does not rain or snow. In the past few years there have been many experiments to try to make rain fall from such clouds. One way tried is to fly an airplane above the clouds and drop bits of dry ice on them. Some of the experiments have worked well. But it is not easy to make rain fall exactly where it is wanted. Besides, all the people in a place never want rain at the same time. (See CLOUDBURST; CLOUDS; HAIL; SNOW; U. S. WEATHER BUREAU; WEATHER.)

RAINBOW After a summer shower there is often a rainbow in the sky. It is made by sunlight shining through tiny drops of water in the air. The tiny drops of water break the sunlight up into the colors it is made of. These colors are violet, indigo, blue, green, yellow, orange, and red. The initial letters of the rainbow colors spell "vibgyor." This is not a real word, but remembering it helps people remember the order of the colors in a rainbow. Some people remember the initial letters by putting them the other way around. Then the letters spell "Roy G. Biv."

The colors in a rainbow shade into one another. It is hard to pick out indigo as dif-

A rainbow often appears at the end of a shower.

ferent from blue. In fact, many people say that there are only six colors in the rainbow. They leave out indigo.

A rainbow disappears as soon as there are no longer any raindrops in the air. The reason that a rainbow usually comes after a shower is that not till then do the clouds begin to break away so that the sun can shine through the raindrops.

A rainbow is always in the part of the sky opposite from the sun. In the morning, when the sun is in the east, a rainbow is always in the west. In the afternoon, when the sun has moved to the west, a rainbow can only appear in the east. There cannot be a rainbow at noon.

Once in a while there is a double rainbow. In an ordinary rainbow red is at the top and violet at the bottom. In a second rainbow the colors are turned around.

Little rainbows can often be seen in the spray of a waterfall. They can even be seen in the spray of a lawn sprinkler.

There is an old saying that there is a pot of gold at the end of the rainbow. Many children have hunted for it. Of course, no one has ever found it. No one could ever get to the end of the rainbow. No matter how far a person traveled toward a rainbow, the rainbow would always be ahead of him.

There are many myths about rainbows. The rainbow, so the myths say, made a bridge by which the gods could come down to earth. (See COLOR; LIGHT.)

Texas, Home of the Longhorn

RANCHES Every boy or girl who likes cowboy stories knows about ranches. For ranches and cowboys go together. Ranches are big farms used chiefly for raising cattle or sheep. They are in parts of the world where the land is good for grass rather than for such crops as corn, wheat, and cotton. In the United States the ranches are in the West and the Southwest. One of these ranches may be so big that it has thousands of cattle or sheep on it. Australia and Canada have big ranches, too.

Ranch buildings are one-story buildings. They fit well into the grasslands. There is no point to having buildings two or three stories high when there is so much open space. People have come to like the low houses on ranches so well that many of the new homes in towns and cities are built like ranch houses.

Airplane Patrolling the Range

Life on a ranch is not as exciting as many stories and motion pictures make it seem. There is much hard work to be done. But many people like it because it keeps them out-of-doors most of the time.

Some ranches are called dude ranches. Many visitors spend vacations at dude ranches. They enjoy riding horseback and being out-of-doors. (See CATTLE; MEAT AND MEAT-PACKING; SHEEP.)

Branding a Calf

"Cookie" and the Chuck Wagon

RAPHAEL (1483-1520) Many great artists have not been called great until after they were dead. Raphael's story is very different. The people of his time recognized him as one of their greatest artists. They called him *divino pittore*, which means "divine painter." The sweetness and charm of his pictures of the mother of Jesus—his Madonnas—won immediate praise. Just as his Madonnas were loved by all kinds of people, the artist was loved by rich and poor, young and old. When he died, such crowds came to his funeral that it seemed all Rome was there.

Raphael—his full name was Raphael Sanzio—was born in Urbino, Italy. His father was a painter and poet. The boy was left an orphan when he was 11. It was clear that Raphael had remarkable talent, and his father had given him lessons in painting. At 16 he entered the workshop of the artist Perugino at Perugia. In almost no time he was painting as well as his master. He began to paint pictures of his own in addition to helping Perugino.

When he was 21, Raphael visited Florence for the first time. At this time two of the greatest artists the world has ever known were living there—Leonardo da Vinci and Michelangelo. When Raphael saw their work he knew that he still had much to learn. And he set about learning it. Raphael, like almost all artists, borrowed from other artists any ideas that would help his own work. From Leonardo he learned about drawing and about making rich patterns. From Michelangelo he learned how important it is for an artist to know the human body thoroughly.

Raphael's visit to Florence was a short one, but he soon returned there to live. He remained almost two years. During these two years he painted many of his most famous Madonnas.

The beauty of these paintings has made them popular all over the world. Today they may be seen in museums in Italy and in Vienna, Madrid, London, Paris, Munich, Berlin, New York, and a few other cities. The most famous Madonna of all, "The Sistine Madonna," was the last one Raphael painted. It is in a museum in Dresden, Germany. A Raphael Madonna is almost always the most popular painting in any museum that has one.

In 1508, at the age of 25, Raphael went to Rome. At that time the cathedral of St. Peter was being built, and the pope was having a great deal of painting done in the Vatican. At the same time Michelangelo was painting the ceiling of the Sistine Chapel, Raphael was at work in the apartments of Pope Julius II. He filled these rooms with magnificent frescoes. Most of these frescoes have either religious or mythological subjects. In these paintings Raphael used the faces of many people living in his own time. In one painting he used his own face.

Raphael did more than paint pictures. Before he was 35 he was doing at least half a dozen different kinds of work. He had become the architect of St. Peter's.

Raphael is famous for his Madonna paintings.

He made plans for private palaces. He had charge of digging up and saving relics of ancient Rome. He designed mosaics and tapestries. And he kept on painting frescoes and portraits. He could not carry out all this work without help. He had about 50 younger artists working with him.

Raphael's work brought him great riches and a high social position. But he did not live long to enjoy them. He was always rather frail, and he was tired from overwork. Late in March of 1520, he caught a fever. He died on April 6, 1520, his 37th birthday. (See MICHELANGELO; PAINTERS AND PAINTING; RENAISSANCE; VINCI, LEONARDO DA.)

Making Rayon

Rayon Threads

Scarf

Tire Cords

Sweater

Rayon, a Man-made Fiber

RATEL The ratel is found in Africa and India. Another name for it is "honey badger." It looks a great deal like a badger, and wild honey is one of its favorite foods. It has long, strong claws that are useful in digging honey out of hollow trees. Its thick fur keeps it from being stung by the bees that it disturbs.

Most animals are darker on top than underneath. The honey badger is just the opposite. Its back is very much lighter than the under part of its body. In fact, the ratel looks as if it were wearing a light blanket on its back. Its color, then, is not a good protection, but it is not important that it should be, for the honey badger sleeps in its burrow during the daytime and goes hunting only at night. It

The ratel seems to wear a gray blanket.

eats rats and other small animals in addition to eating honey. Little birds called honey guides are sometimes a help to ratels in finding honey. The honey guides fly to trees where they have found young bees to eat, and the ratels follow them.

The African natives are very much afraid of this animal. It is fearless, and it is very strong for its size. Men who have tried to ship honey badgers to zoos have found that they can claw their way out of any box that is not lined with metal.

RAYON Up till nearly the beginning of the 20th century all cloth was woven out of fibers from plants or animals. By far the most beautiful fiber was silk. But it was expensive. A great many people could never afford clothes made of silk. And no other cloth looked at all like it.

Now there are other kinds of cloth that look much like silk. And some of them are much less expensive. They are woven of man-made fibers. The oldest of these man-made fibers is rayon.

A French scientist, Count Hilaire de Chardonnet, began making rayon in 1891. The materials he used were wood pulp and cotton. With chemicals he changed the wood pulp and cotton into a thick liquid that looked like honey. He squeezed this liquid through holes the size of a pinpoint. It came out in fine threads. The threads were bathed with a chemical which hardened them. Then they were twisted into thicker threads, or yarn. This could be woven into cloth.

The new fiber was not called rayon at first. It was called artificial silk. It did not get the name rayon until about 25 years later, after it had crossed the ocean and was being made in the United States.

No one liked rayon much in the beginning. It did not look like real silk. Soon, however, it was improved. By the time it got the name rayon it was beginning to be popular. Today millions of pounds of rayon are made and sold every year.

There are now different kinds of rayon. They are all made of wood pulp and cotton. The cotton used is the "fuzz" left on the seeds after the longer cotton fibers have been taken off. The cotton and wood can be changed into a liquid by using different chemicals. There are different ways of making the fine threads into yarn, too.

One kind of rayon that is very well liked now is the kind that is called rayon acetate, or acetate for short. Many of the ready-made clothes we buy today have a label in them that says "acetate."

Rayon can be dyed many beautiful colors. It will keep its beauty for a long time if it is well taken care of. It must never be pressed with a very hot iron.

There are many newer man-made fibers. But they have not crowded out rayon. (See FIBERS; SILK; TEXTILES.)

REBUS A rebus is a kind of riddle. It is a story that is written partly in pictures. A picture may stand for a whole word or it may stand for only a part of a word.

The answer to this rebus is: Someone saw many people race by. They would not stop to tell why they were all in a rush.

RED SEA The Red Sea really is red. It gets its color from billions of tiny red plants called algae that grow in it.

The Red Sea is an arm of the Indian Ocean between Africa and Arabia. Only a narrow strip of land separates it from the Mediterranean. The Suez Canal now crosses this strip of land. One of the world's most important ocean routes goes from the Mediterranean through the Suez Canal into the Red Sea. From there it goes on to the Far East. (See SUEZ CANAL.)

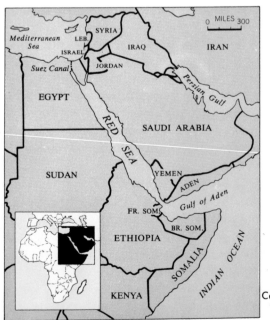

Camel

Arab

Oil Port

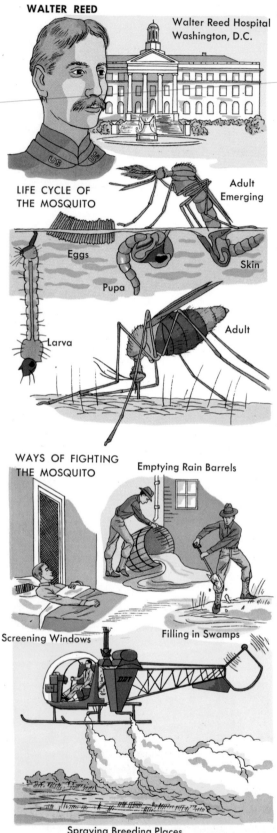

WALTER REED

Walter Reed Hospital
Washington, D.C.

LIFE CYCLE OF
THE MOSQUITO

Adult
Emerging

Eggs

Skin

Pupa

Larva

Adult

WAYS OF FIGHTING
THE MOSQUITO

Emptying Rain Barrels

Screening Windows

Filling in Swamps

Spraying Breeding Places

REED, WALTER (1851-1902) In a way Walter Reed was a detective. For he succeeded in tracking down two public enemies. He found out that the common housefly carries typhoid fever and that one kind of mosquito carries yellow fever.

As a boy Walter Reed lived in Virginia. His father was a minister there. Walter was only 16 when he entered the University of Virginia. He knew that he wanted to study medicine. But he knew, too, that his father could not pay for the many years of study it usually took to become a doctor. He therefore asked the officials of the university whether he could take the examinations as soon as he thought he was ready. They agreed, never dreaming that he would be able to pass them in nine months. But he was. He was the youngest student ever to graduate from the medical school of the University of Virginia.

After a few years in New York, Reed became an army doctor. He was sent to a garrison in Arizona. Just before he left for his new post he was married.

For 14 years he stayed in Arizona. He doctored not only the soldiers of the garrison but all the sick people round about. The life was hard, especially since there were unfriendly Indians in the region.

From Arizona Reed was sent to Baltimore. He had a chance to study in the famous Johns Hopkins University there. Soon he became a professor himself in the Army Medical School in Washington. His first big job was to find out why there was so much typhoid fever in army camps. He found out that flies were partly to blame because they were carrying germs to the food the soldiers ate.

At that time yellow fever was even more of a problem than typhoid. It was very common in Cuba and Central America and there had been many epidemics of it in cities in the United States. Thousands of people had died in those epidemics. In 1900 Reed and several other army doctors were sent to Cuba to study this disease.

Already many clues pointed to mosquitoes as the carriers of yellow fever. Reed thought the clues were good. But the only way to find out was to let some mosquitoes bite some people sick with yellow fever and then let them bite some well ones. Several brave people offered to let themselves be bitten. They knew that they might get the disease and might die. Three of them did get the disease, but they all got well. A little while later, however, Dr. Lazear, one of the doctors working with Reed, was bitten while he was visiting a yellow fever hospital. He saw the mosquito but did not try to kill it when it settled on the back of his hand. He got the disease and died.

More experimenting made Reed sure that only mosquitoes could carry yellow fever. The way to get rid of yellow fever was then clear—get rid of the mosquitoes.

In Havana, Cuba, a campaign to destroy mosquitoes brought an end to yellow fever there. Killing mosquitoes did away with yellow fever in other places, too. Today there is little of it.

Reed died soon after he saw Havana free from yellow fever. He had appendicitis. To help people remember him and the work he did the government named a big army hospital in Washington, D.C. for him — the Walter Reed Hospital. (See DISEASES; MOSQUITO; PANAMA CANAL.)

REFRIGERATORS Long ago people found that keeping foods cool helps keep them from spoiling. Besides, many foods taste better when they are cold. Refrigerators, therefore, are important.

The first refrigerators were simple iceboxes. Ice was cut from lakes and ponds in the winter and stored in deep pits or in ice houses to be used in the summertime. An icebox was built to hold a cake of ice in one part and food in another part. As the ice melted, it cooled the air around it. The food in turn, was cooled by the air. As soon as one block of ice melted, another was put in. At first only the people in regions with cold winters could have iceboxes. But ways of making artificial ice were discovered. Then even in warm regions people could have iceboxes.

Now mechanical refrigerators have almost crowded out iceboxes. Most of us use fans to cool ourselves on a hot day. Fanning cools us because it makes the perspiration evaporate faster. A mechanical refrigerator makes use of the fact that evaporation is cooling.

Many mechanical refrigerators are run by electricity. The one in the picture is an electric refrigerator. It works in this way: A liquid evaporates very fast in the cooling coils. This liquid is called a refrigerant. As it evaporates it takes heat away from the food in the refrigerator. It makes the water in the freezing trays freeze into ice cubes. After the liquid evaporates, the gas formed goes to a compressor and then to a condenser. They change the gas back to a liquid. The liquid returns to the cooling coils and evaporates again. The same refrigerant is used over and over. An electric motor drives the compressor.

A Deepfreeze is a mechanical refrigerator in which the temperature is kept below freezing. Evaporation must go on faster than in an ordinary refrigerator. (See AIR CONDITIONING.)

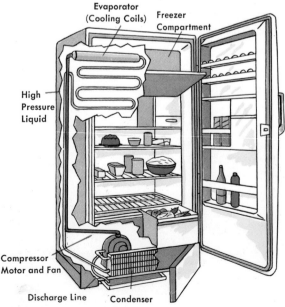

Evaporator (Cooling Coils)
Freezer Compartment
High Pressure Liquid
Compressor Motor and Fan
Discharge Line
Condenser

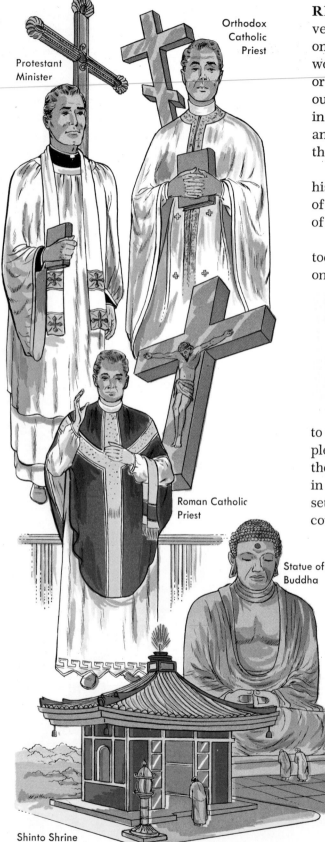

Protestant Minister

Orthodox Catholic Priest

Roman Catholic Priest

Statue of Buddha

Shinto Shrine

Star of David

The Torah

Jewish Rabbi

Moslems Praying

RELIGIONS OF THE WORLD From very early times people have believed in one god or in more than one. They have worked out ways of worshiping the god or gods they believed in. They have worked out beliefs in what is right and wrong and in what comes after death. Their beliefs and their ways of worshiping make up their religion.

There have been many religions in the history of the world. Some of the religions of today have only a few followers. Some of them have millions.

This list names the leading religions of today and tells how many followers each one of them has.

Buddhism	150,000,000
Christianity	820,000,000
Confucianism	300,000,000
Hinduism	319,000,000
Islam	417,000,000
Judaism	12,000,000
Shintoism	30,000,000
Taoism	50,000,000

Wars have been fought to force people to worship in a certain way. And some people have been badly treated because of their religion. Religion played a big part in the settling of the United States. Many settlers were seeking a place where they could worship in their own way.

Rembrandt Working on "The Night Watch"

REMBRANDT VAN RIJN (1606-1669)
Rembrandt, one of the greatest artists of all time, was born in Leyden in the Netherlands. His family ground its own grain in a windmill on the city's wall. As a child he liked to sketch the sun coming in a tiny window and making a streak of light on the inside of the windmill. He carried this interest in light and shadow through life. His paintings often show one hand of a person in the light and one in the dark.

Many artists traveled to faraway lands. Rembrandt always stayed within 50 miles of his home, although he lived to be 63.

Much of his life was spent in Amsterdam, then the richest town in Europe. In some of Rembrandt's paintings we see the rich clothes and jewels worn by people of that time in Amsterdam.

During the first ten years of his career he was a famous and fashionable painter. Then something happened which ruined him. He became so poor that he had to sell all his furniture and even his rich velvet clothes. To make matters worse, his wealthy wife died, and her parents took the money she had left to him.

This was what happened to ruin the sale of his paintings: The Amsterdam Civic Guard had paid him to paint a picture of them. Since he liked light and shadow, he painted the men as they were leaving the armory at noon to go on duty. The men still inside were in such deep shadow that their faces could not be recognized. These men were very angry. The men in the sunlight of course showed well. But their satisfaction did not make up for the anger of the others. The picture is one of Rembrandt's best. It is called "The Night Watch," although it was painted at noon.

Even poverty did not keep Rembrandt from painting. He married a girl who had been a nurse for his son. They had a daughter. Since Rembrandt was too poor to hire models, he painted his wife, his daughter, and, with the help of a mirror, himself. He painted the poor, the lame, the blind, and the sick. He dressed them in Biblical costumes, as was often done in his time.

Other Dutch artists of the time painted cloth of lovely texture, dishes, tiles, and other such things simply because they were beautiful. They painted pictures of rooms with handsomely dressed people in them. Rembrandt was greater because he painted people so that we can tell how they felt and thought. He painted their personalities, not just their clothes.

Rembrandt worked hard all his life becoming a better and better artist. The world stopped paying him. The people of his time stopped honoring him. But he was far greater than they. He was a great artist working on art problems ahead of his time. (See PAINTERS AND PAINTING.)

Armor Making

Copernicus Scientific Discovery

Columbus Exploring

St. Peter's Cathedral

Catherine De Medici Patroness of Art

The Renaissance was an exciting age of painters, writers, explorers, scientists, and scholars.

RENAISSANCE A period of about 250 years in Europe's history is called the Renaissance. The name "Renaissance" means "rebirth." What was reborn was an interest in the arts and in learning.

For several hundred "dark" years after the fall of the Roman Empire, civilization in Europe in some ways went backward. Most of the writings of the Greeks and the Romans were forgotten. There were very few scholars and artists. There were no strong governments. Fighting or working hard to get a bare living filled the lives of most men of the time.

But little by little the people of Europe climbed out of their age of darkness. Finally the interest in learning and art was so great that in later centuries the age was given the name of the Renaissance.

Since the new birth of interest in learning and art was gradual, it is hard to say exactly when the Renaissance began. Some people think that the best date for its beginning is the date when printing was invented in Europe—about the middle of the 15th century. It is certainly true that the invention of printing gave interest in learning a great boost.

The Renaissance began in Italy. From there it spread over the rest of Europe. New interest in the writings of the ancient Greeks and Romans was a part of it. But the "rebirth" spread into other fields from literature—into art and music, and into science and exploration. Among the great names of the Renaissance are writers, painters, sculptors, scholars, explorers, and scientists. Some rulers, moreover, played an important role.

Of the rulers, Lorenzo the Magnificent was one of the most colorful. He was for many years the ruler of Florence, in Italy. His help encouraged a number of artists and writers who became famous. Leonardo da Vinci, painter, inventor, and one of the great men of all time, belongs in the Renaissance. So does Erasmus, a truly great scholar. Michelangelo, Raphael, Titian, Holbein, Andrea del Sarto, Copernicus, Vasco da Gama, Columbus, and Shakespeare are a few of the other "greats" of this age.

The Renaissance did not have any sudden ending, just as it did not have any sudden beginning. The death of the famous Queen Elizabeth I of England in 1603 is sometimes given as the end of the period.

Of course the interest in art and learning did not end with the end of the period. But other interests were added. The development of trade and the settlement of the

Painting

Sometimes Renoir traveled to other countries — to Algeria, for instance — where the sun was very bright and the flowers were brilliant red, orange, blue, and violet. After painting in sunny climates he remembered the colors he saw there and used them in other scenes. His colors are often called jewellike.

When some artists use bright colors together they look cheap. Renoir's colors never look cheap, partly because he studied the science of color.

When Renoir painted human flesh, it looked warm and alive. When he painted eyes, they looked very bright. Renoir used lovely colors in his paintings, and he painted happy subjects.

When Renoir first began to paint pictures he painted in a style which was later followed by other painters—the Impressionists. He soon, however, outgrew this style of painting. The Impressionists put red and blue next to each other in a painting and let the eyes of the people who looked at the painting mix them into purple. They put blue and yellow next to each other and let people's eyes mix them into green. The Impressionists were more interested in light than in form. Renoir grew to like form. In his paintings the people look real—they do not look as if they were made of cardboard.

New World were two of them. In many, many ways the people of Europe today are better off than they were during the Renaissance. But it must have been a thrilling time to those who lived in it. (See COLUMBUS, CHRISTOPHER; COPERNICUS; DARK AGES; ELIZABETH I; EXPLORERS; GUTENBERG, JOHANN; MICHELANGELO; MIDDLE AGES; PAINTERS AND PAINTING; RAPHAEL; SHAKESPEARE, WILLIAM; VINCI, LEONARDO DA.)

RENOIR, PIERRE AUGUSTE (1841-1919) Among French painters Renoir ranks high. When Renoir was a boy he painted on white porcelain to earn money for his food and clothing. He painted with very brilliant colors. Even though he was working for his living he enjoyed every minute of his painting because he could work with bright colors.

Renoir never lost his love for color. He continually experimented with it when he grew to manhood and became a painter of pictures. He often began a picture by painting a scene or person in his own town so that his drawing would be right. But he then finished the picture with colors far more brilliant than the colors he saw in his surroundings.

Renoir often painted pictures of little girls.

The largest dinosaurs were the largest land animals that ever lived.

REPTILES A hundred million years ago there were many more reptiles than there are now. They were everywhere—on land, in the air, and in the sea. There were so many of them that this bygone age is now called the Age of Reptiles.

Many of the kinds of reptiles that lived during the Age of Reptiles can no longer be found. Even the dinosaurs, which once ruled the earth, are all gone.

The reptiles living now are divided into five groups. The pictures show one reptile from each of the five groups. The two best-known groups are the snakes and the turtles. Snakes are known by their shape and turtles by their shells. The alligators and crocodiles are larger but are not found in so many places. Lizards are close relatives of the snakes. They look quite different, however, because most lizards have legs. The tuatara is in a group by itself. This

reptile is found only on some small islands near New Zealand.

The word "reptile" comes from a Latin word meaning "to creep." Whether they have short legs or no legs at all, reptiles move chiefly by creeping.

Although many reptiles spend much time in water, they are really land animals. They have lungs, and most of them depend on land life for food. Reptiles are covered with dry scales. They are not slimy.

Most reptiles lay eggs. Those that do, lay their eggs on land. The eggs are well protected by a tough outer covering. A few reptiles are live-bearing—that is, their young are born live, not hatched.

All reptiles, like fishes and amphibians and unlike birds and mammals, are cold blooded. Therefore, reptiles that live in lands with cold winters must hibernate.

A few reptiles are used for food. The leatherlike coverings of some are used for making such things as purses, shoes, and belts. But reptiles as a group are far less important to us than fishes, mammals, and birds. (See ALLIGATORS AND CROCODILES; DINOSAURS; LEATHER; LIFE THROUGH THE AGES; LIZARDS; SNAKES; TURTLES.)

Green Turtle

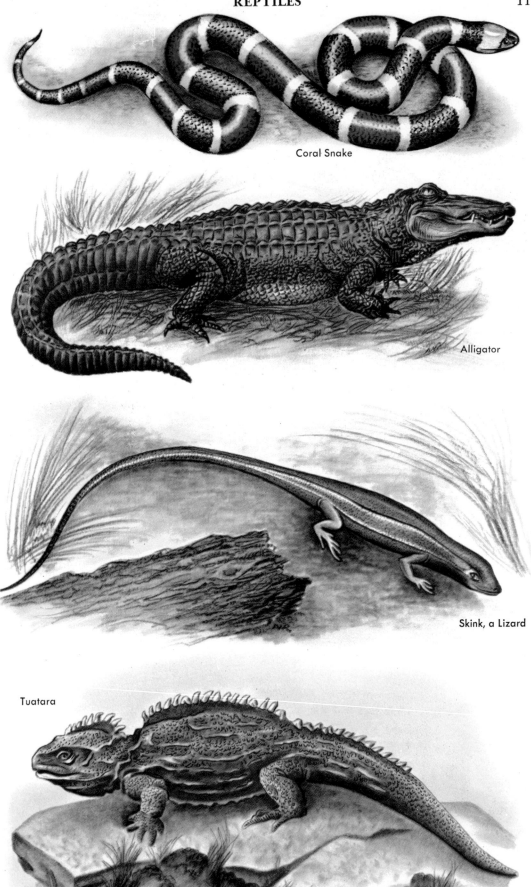

Coral Snake

Alligator

Skink, a Lizard

Tuatara

Paul Revere saw the warning lights in the tower.

REVERE, PAUL (1735-1818) Among early American silversmiths, Paul Revere ranks high. But probably not many people today would ever hear of him if it had not been for his famous midnight ride.

Revere lived in Boston in the days when the people of the American colonies were beginning to rebel against English rule. He belonged to a group of patriots and had taken part in the Boston Tea Party. This "tea party" was a warning that the colonists would refuse to pay taxes unless they had some share in their own government.

In 1775 there were British troops in Boston ready to enforce the orders of the English king. The colonists, knowing that they might have to fight for their freedom, had ammunition stored at Concord, near Boston. They also had some soldiers called minutemen who went about their regular work but were ready to shoulder their guns at a minute's notice.

The group of patriots Revere belonged to found out that the British soldiers were planning to march on Concord to seize the ammunition. But no one knew whether they would march by land or go by water. It was important that the minutemen be told as soon as possible how the troops were coming. Of course, there were no telephones or telegraphs or radios then. Paul Revere agreed to spread the news over the countryside as soon as it was known.

Night after night he had his horse saddled and waiting while he watched for a signal. The signal was to be given by lantern from the tower of Old North Church in Boston. One lighted lantern would mean that the British were coming by land, two that they were coming by water.

On the night of the 18th of April, 1775, Revere saw two lanterns flash from the church tower. He was off at once, and with the help of another rider, he soon spread the news. When the British reached Concord, they found the minutemen ready to fight, and the Revolutionary War began.

Revere was a soldier all during the war. Then he went back to Boston and his work as a silversmith.

The poet Longfellow told the story of Paul Revere's midnight ride in a poem that almost every American has read. Revere's house is now one of the sights of Old Boston. (See UNITED STATES HISTORY.)

RHINE RIVER The picture shows a scene on the famous river Rhine. It is not an unusual scene, for terraced hillsides covered with vineyards stretch for miles along the Middle Rhine. And there are many centuries-old castles on the heights.

No river has more legends about it than the Rhine. One legend tells of a beautiful maiden, the Lorelei, who was supposed to sit on a rock in the middle of the river, combing her beautiful golden hair and luring sailors to their death. Another legend tells that at Bingen on the Rhine mice once killed a hated bishop. A tower there is called the "Mouse Tower."

A Castle on the Rhine

The Rhine rises in Switzerland. It flows northward for more than 800 miles into the North Sea. For most of its length it is in Germany or on its border. But its mouths—it has several, just as the Mississippi has—are in the Netherlands.

During the Middle Ages the Rhine was a very busy highway. It still is. No other river in Europe carries so many thousands of tons of cargo. Canals connect it with many other rivers. Barges loaded with coal, iron, oil, and other bulky materials are constantly traveling up and down the Rhine and from it to other parts of Europe.

Rotterdam, Düsseldorf, and Cologne are three of the cities that have grown up on the Lower Rhine. Rotterdam is in the Netherlands. Düsseldorf and Cologne are in Germany. The Ruhr River enters the Rhine just below these two cities. The Ruhr region is one of the busiest parts of Europe. Coal mines, steel mills, and factories crowd the banks of the Ruhr. Cities are so close together, they seem almost one city.

The Rhine with its traffic from the Ruhr is indeed a busy working river. Even so, hundreds of tourists enjoy its charm from river steamers. Many stop at Bonn, West Germany's capital city. (See CASTLES; GERMANY; NETHERLANDS.)

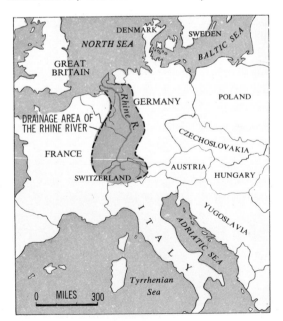

African Rhinoceros

RHINOCEROS The name "rhinoceros" comes from Greek words meaning "nose" and "horn." Every rhinoceros has at least one horn on its nose. It may have two.

A rhinoceros is a big, thick-skinned animal. Although it is a mammal, it has almost no hair on its skin. The eyes of a rhinoceros are small. The animal has poor sight. Its senses of hearing and smell, however, are keen.

Rhinoceroses are found in southern Asia, the East Indies, and Africa. The rhinoceros usually seen in zoos is the Indian rhinoceros. This rhinoceros has heavy folds of skin across its back. It has only one horn, which is about a foot long. For centuries this horn has been used by the Chinese in certain medicines.

The white rhinoceros of Africa, which has two horns, is the largest of the rhinoceroses. Of all land animals only the elephant and the hippopotamus are larger. The white rhinoceros is really gray, not white. But at a distance it may look almost white because of the dried mud on its body. It often wallows in mud to get relief from mosquitoes and other insects.

The white rhinoceros has bird companions. These birds seem to give warning when danger is near.

If a rhinoceros is disturbed, it usually goes off at a fast trot. To defend itself, however, a rhinoceros may charge head down at its enemy. It is then dangerous.

RHODE ISLAND "Little Rhody" is the smallest state in the United States. It is one of the oldest states, too. In earlier times, Rhode Island was one of the famous 13 American colonies that became the first 13 states. In 1936, Rhode Islanders celebrated the 300th anniversary of the founding of Providence, the first settlement in that colony. Today, Providence is the state's capital and largest city.

Tiny Rhode Island is tucked in between Connecticut to the west and Massachusetts to the north and east. It is bordered on the south by the Atlantic. As the map shows, a long bay called Narragansett Bay is in the eastern part of the state.

Rhode Island is the name of the largest island in that bay. That name is only a part of the state's whole name. Its real name, which is on the state seal, is so long that it is hardly ever used. It is "Rhode Island and Providence Plantations." Providence Plantations is a name given long ago to the mainland in the colony. Little Rhody's long name suggests, then, that both islands and mainland make up the state. From 1854 until 1901, Rhode Island had two capitals—the cities of Providence on the mainland and Newport on the *island* of Rhode Island.

One of the most famous of the early settlers was Roger Williams. He and some of the other settlers had been banished from Massachusetts because they complained about not having enough freedom there. He paid the Indians for land he got from them. At first, settlers depended chiefly on fishing and the few crops they could raise. But before the American Revolution, Rhode Island had 350 trading vessels sailing from Newfoundland to Georgia. Some went on much longer trading voyages. In 1790, Samuel Slater, a factory worker from England, built at Pawtucket the first power machinery in America for spinning cotton yarn. Cotton mills and mill towns sprang up where falls in rivers furnished power.

Important among Rhode Island's factory products today are textiles, machinery, jewelry, and silverware. Providence, Pawtucket, Cranston, and Woonsocket are among its larger manufacturing cities. Over four-fifths of the Rhode Islanders now live in cities or towns. In the last 100 years, thousands of people from Europe have come to find work in Rhode Island.

Only about 2 out of every 100 people in the state are farmers. They produce food city people want to have fresh—eggs, dairy products, vegetables, and chickens. Rhode Island Red poultry is famous.

There are as many people in Rhode Island as there are in each of 13 larger states. But in spite of its many crowded areas, there are many handsome colonial and modern homes, much forest land, many beauty spots, and many lovely beaches and vacation resorts. The city of Newport has long been a famous resort. Near Newport, too, is the Naval War College. In September of 1958, the famous yacht races for the America's Cup were held off Newport and brought many visitors to Rhode Island's shores. The tiny state of Rhode Island and Providence Plantations is a remarkable little state. (See CONNECTICUT; MASSACHUSETTS; NEW ENGLAND; YACHTS AND YACHTING.)

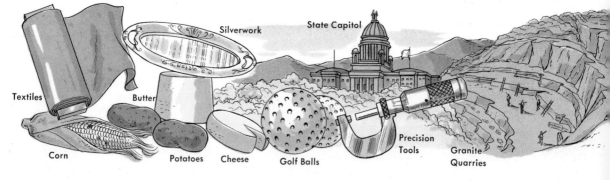

Textiles Silverwork Butter State Capitol Precision Tools Granite Quarries Corn Potatoes Cheese Golf Balls

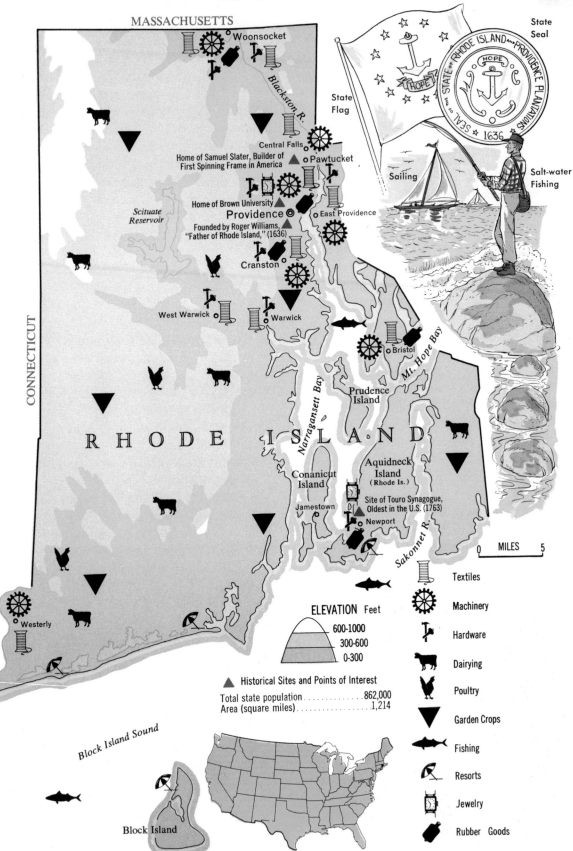

MASSACHUSETTS

Woonsocket

Blackston R.

Central Falls

Home of Samuel Slater, Builder of
First Spinning Frame in America

Pawtucket

CONNECTICUT

Scituate
Reservoir

Home of Brown University

Providence

East Providence

Founded by Roger Williams,
"Father of Rhode Island," (1636)

Cranston

West Warwick   Warwick

Bristol

Narragansett Bay

Prudence
Island

Mt. Hope Bay

R H O D E   I S L A N D

Aquidneck
Island
(Rhode Is.)

Conanicut
Island

Site of Touro Synagogue,
Oldest in the U.S. (1763)

Jamestown

Newport

Sakonnet R.

Westerly

State
Flag

State
Seal

Sailing

Salt-water
Fishing

MILES   5
0

ELEVATION Feet
600-1000
300-600
0-300

Historical Sites and Points of Interest

Total state population 862,000
Area (square miles) 1,214

Textiles

Machinery

Hardware

Dairying

Poultry

Garden Crops

Fishing

Resorts

Jewelry

Rubber Goods

Block Island Sound

Block Island

RICE Fields of rice are as common in some parts of the world as fields of corn or wheat are in the United States. The people of southern China, Japan, India, the Philippines, and southeastern Asia live chiefly on this cereal. Some rice is raised in southern United States, but it is not one of the more important crops there.

Rice has been a common food for many centuries. We know that it has been raised in some places for more than 4,000 years.

A field of rice ready for harvest looks from a distance much like a field of ripe wheat. It is not surprising that it does, for rice and wheat are rather close relatives. They both belong to the big family of grasses, the plant family that gives us all our cereal grains.

Rice needs more warmth and much more water than most crops. Most rice fields are kept flooded a large part of the time while the rice is growing. The flooded fields are drained when the rice is about ready to be harvested.

Rice grains are mostly starch. Some rice is made into flour. Rice flour is not good for making loaves of bread. But it is often used for making thin cakes a little like crackers. Most rice is boiled and eaten with a meal much as Americans eat potatoes.

The white rice we buy in grocery stores has been polished—the brown hull of the grain has been taken off. Polished rice is not nearly as good for us as unpolished rice, for the hull has vitamins and minerals in it. If the people who live mostly on rice eat polished rice, they are likely to have the disease called beriberi. This disease is caused by a lack of vitamin B_1.

The Japanese drink called sake (SAH ke) is made from rice. Other peoples make other drinks from this grain. Rice straw can be woven into hats, shoes, and matting. (See CEREALS; FOODS; GRASSES; MINERALS; VITAMINS.)

RIO DE JANEIRO Whether approaching by ship or air, visitors to Rio de Janeiro are struck by the great beauty of this famous city of Brazil. Mountains look down like giants at a toy town. Tropical vegetation covers the mountains almost to the top. A granite peak rises near the entrance to the roomy bay which Rio borders. This peak, as tall as the Empire State Building in New York City, is called Sugar Loaf Mountain.

Many visitors ride a cable car to the top of Sugar Loaf or take a cog railroad to the top of another peak nearby, which is nearly twice as high. From such high points they see how Rio has been built into its gorgeous setting. Following the shoreline for many miles are sandy beaches. Long rows of tall

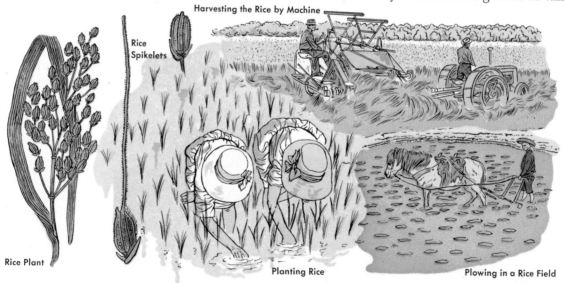

Harvesting the Rice by Machine

Rice Spikelets

Rice Plant

Planting Rice

Plowing in a Rice Field

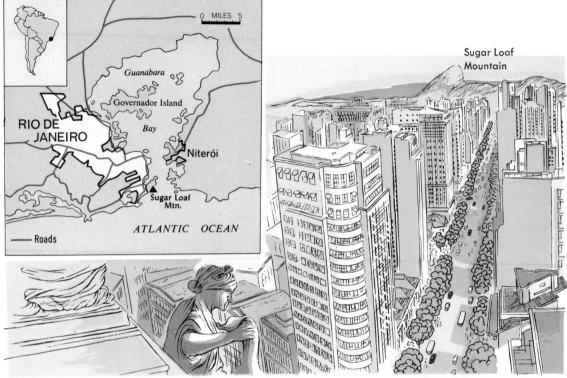

Street in Rio

apartment buildings, hotels, and fine homes line the broad highway near the shore.

It is several miles from the entrance of the Bay to the docks of this busy seaport. A huge airport is on level land at the waterfront here. A mountain was cut down and millions of tons of rock dumped into the Bay to make land for the airport. Not far away are the tall buildings of the city's modern business district.

Except for the downtown district Rio does not spread out. Instead it reaches long arms up narrow valleys and into the hills and mountains. Tunnels have been bored through the mountains in places to make it easier for people to get from one section of the city to another.

Rio has many fine, tree-shaded avenues lined with beautiful buildings. One of these avenues is the Avenida Rio Branco. It is along this broad avenue that the big parade of Rio's famous Carnival moves. The Carnival is held the four days before the beginning of Lent each year. It is a time of fun for everyone. Grownups and children alike dress up in gay costumes. Clowns, goblins, pirates, and pixies all join together in the songs and dances.

Many kinds of work keep the people of Rio busy. Wholesale houses, transportation terminals, assembly plants, and factories need many workers. Rio is a good place for factories. Mountain streams drive big power plants to give electricity for the factories. Metal goods, furniture, and cloth are among the things made. Salvador was the capital of Brazil until 1763, when Rio was made the capital city. Many government offices are located in Rio and many of Rio's people are government workers.

It is more than 400 years since some Portuguese seamen sailed into the Bay on a summer New Year's Day. They thought they had reached the mouth of a large river and named it River of January. The city took that name. Rio now has more than 2,500,000 people. But it is no longer Brazil's largest city. In recent years São Paulo has grown so fast that it now has more people than Rio. (See BRAZIL.)

Glacier

Lake

Canyon

Evaporation

Gap

River

Stream

River
Mouth

Delta

Oce

THE STORY OF A RIVER

RIVERS In a steep cliff on the edge of the sea a tiny gully starts. After a rain, water rushes down the gully into the sea. The water rushing down wears the gully deeper. Little by little water running into it at its head makes the gully longer, too.

As the gully gets deeper and longer, it also gets wider. It swallows up other gullies near by. At last it gets so wide and so long and so deep that it has water in it all the time. It is now the valley of a little stream.

The stream slowly grows large enough to be called a river. The young river eats its way farther and farther back into the land. Little gullies on its banks grow into stream valleys. Their streams become branches of the river. The river gradually makes its valley wider. At first its valley is shaped like a capital *V*. Now it begins to have a flat floor. The river becomes middle-aged. It is many miles long.

The river now cuts sideways faster than it cuts down. Its valley becomes very wide.

The river wanders back and forth over it, flowing slowly. It is now an old river.

This story is the story of most rivers. A river is young, then middle-aged, then old. Its valley tells its age. Strangely enough, a young river may be many times as old in years as an old river. For example, a river that is cutting its way through soft rock or soil grows old much faster than a river that is cutting through very hard rock. The Colorado River, which flows through the Grand Canyon, has been flowing on its way for millions of years, but it is still young. Its valley is still V-shaped.

No one in his lifetime sees a river "grow up." The great rivers of the world were thousands of years in the making.

Rivers have always been highways. Probably people floated down them on rafts made of logs even before they knew how to make boats. There were river highways long before there were good roads, and even longer before there were railroads. In some parts of the world the best way of traveling is still on the rivers. In fact, many of the world's largest cities are on rivers. Some of these cities are built where a river meets the sea.

A river is always at work. It may carry logs down mountainsides or turn wheels that drive machines. It may carry wastes away from cities. Its current may move rafts and barges.

But even if a river is not doing any work for people, it is always doing work of its own. It carries loads of soil toward the sea. Water that runs over fields on the way to a stream picks up soil and carries it along to the stream. Besides, the river is always wearing away its banks. Every year rivers dump millions of tons of soil into the sea.

Rivers build new land, too. They build new land by dropping the loads they are carrying when they reach the sea.

But rivers wear away land much faster than they build new land. If rivers were the only forces at work to change the face of the earth, all the land would sooner or later be worn down to the level of the sea.

Some of the world's rivers are thousands of miles long. It is hard to tell exactly how long a river is. A river usually turns and twists. Or it may broaden out into a lake in some places. Should the lake be counted in the length of the river? People do not agree. Besides, it is sometimes hard to tell which is the main river and which is a branch. It is easy to see, then, why different books may give different lengths for the same river.

The Mississippi River is one of the world's great rivers. It flows from northern Minnesota into the Gulf of Mexico. The Missouri River is one of its branches. The Missouri joins the Mississippi near St. Louis. The Missouri measures much longer than the Mississippi from the mouth of the Missouri northward. The Mississippi from the Gulf to the mouth of the Missouri plus the Missouri is one of the longest, if not quite the longest, rivers in the world.

The Seine flows through the center of Paris, France.

The chart below shows 15 of the world's great rivers.

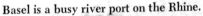

RIVER	FLOWS INTO	LOCATION	LENGTH IN MILES
Nile	Mediterranean	Eastern Africa	4,037
Missouri-Mississippi	Gulf of Mexico	United States	3,988
Amazon	Atlantic Ocean	Brazil	3,690
Ob	Gulf of Ob (Arctic)	U.S.S.R. (Asia)	3,200
Yangtze Kiang	East China Sea	China	3,200
Congo	Atlantic Ocean	Belgian Congo (Africa)	3,000
Lena	Arctic Ocean	U.S.S.R. (Asia)	3,000
Amur	Sea of Okhotsk (Pacific)	U.S.S.R.–China	2,800
Yenisei	Arctic Ocean	U.S.S.R. (Asia)	2,800
Paraná-La Plata	Atlantic Ocean	Brazil-Argentina	2,720
Hwang Ho	Yellow Sea	China	2,700
Mekong	South China Sea	China-Indochina	2,600
Niger	Gulf of Guinea (Atlantic)	Western Africa	2,600
Mackenzie	Beaufort Sea (Arctic)	Canada	2,525
Volga	Caspian Sea	U.S.S.R. (Europe)	2,325

Basel is a busy river port on the Rhine.

Old Roman Road of Stones

ROADS AND STREETS The story of roads begins far back in the days when traveling by foot was the only way of traveling on land. The very first roads were footpaths. Probably people simply took over trails made by wild animals. There are still places where roads are merely footpaths. There are still streets— roads through towns and cities—that are wide enough only for people on foot.

After horses and donkeys were tamed, roads had to be wide enough for riders to pass. Later they had to be wide enough for carts and chariots. In time coaches and big wagons called for still wider roads. In recent years automobiles, buses, and trucks have made the need for wide highways far greater than ever before.

A great many of today's roads and streets are paved. The idea of paving highways is not new. More than 3,000 years ago Babylonia, Egypt, and Crete had some paved highways. But the Romans were the first great builders of paved roads.

Much was learned about the streets of ancient Roman cities when the ruins of the little city of Pompeii were uncovered. The streets there are paved with blocks of stone. At the sides there are raised walks for people on foot, and now and then there are raised stepping stones across the streets. Clearly these Roman streets were planned more for people on foot than for wheeled vehicles.

It is easy to see what Roman roads outside the cities were like, for some of them are still in use. The famous Appian Way is one. The Romans made roads chiefly so they could move their armies quickly.

In the Middle Ages, just as in the days of Rome, most of the wheeled traffic was on the roads outside the cities. Almost the the only travel inside the medieval cities of Europe was on foot or on horseback. Many of the streets were just narrow passageways between the houses. There were seldom any sidewalks.

During the Middle Ages almost no paved roads were built. Roads were so poor even in the 17th century that journeying by horseback was likely to be safer and more comfortable than journeying in a wheeled vehicle. There is a record of a French traveler whose coach was stuck in the mud so often that it took him three full days to travel 20 miles. No wonder most people never traveled far from home!

As trade between cities increased, more attention was paid to streets and roads. Paved highways were built again.

Many different ideas for paving streets and roads have been used. In the early days of the United States, for example, road builders paved roads by laying trunks of trees side by side across the roads. Roads paved in this way were called corduroy roads. It is easy to imagine how bumpy a ride on a corduroy road must have been. The roads of ancient Rome were paved with slabs of stone lying on beds of crushed stone or gravel. Brick, cobblestones, wooden blocks and planks, and asphalt are other materials that have been used.

Good modern road building began about 1800. Then two Englishmen, Thomas Telford and John MacAdam began building roads of crushed stone. Later asphalt or coal tar was added to make macadam roads. The chief road-building material today is concrete. There are now hundreds of thousands of miles of concrete highways in the United States alone.

A great deal of money is now spent on streets and roads. Old highways are re-paved and wonderful new ones are built. Some of the new highways run right through mountains, over and under rivers, or across swamps. In road building today special attention is paid to places where two or more roads cross.

Good roads are so expensive that some roads are being made to pay for themselves through tolls. Every person who travels on such a road must pay a toll, or fee. Roads that are not toll roads are built and kept up through taxes.

Almost as long as there have been roads, some rules of the road have been needed. Suppose, several thousand years ago, two travelers met on a narrow footpath. Should one move aside and let the other have the whole road? Or should each one move aside a little? Gradually customs grew up, and rules grew out of the customs. In the United States, for instance, it is the rule that on a two-way road or street, one keeps to the right side.

Perhaps the right-hand custom came about when people drove oxen along the roads. Oxen were often driven by a person walking beside them at the left. It was therefore more convenient for the driver to move his oxen to the right when he met someone. Even if the oxen had to get off the road, the driver could stay on it.

In England the opposite rule is followed. Traffic keeps to the left. Perhaps this cus-

Dirt Road

Cobblestone Street

Black Top Road

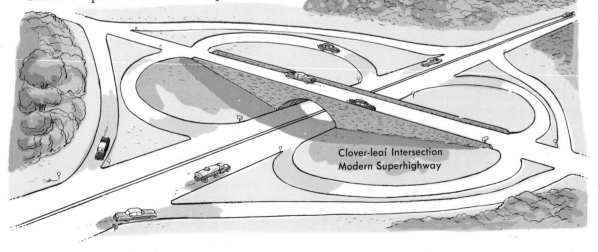

Clover-leaf Intersection
Modern Superhighway

tom came about when men carried swords as they rode about. If a rider was on the left side of the road, his sword arm was toward the approaching traveler.

Today there are many traffic rules. Some of them had to be made in a hurry as automobiles began to crowd the highways. There was no chance to wait till rules could grow up from customs. Signals of many kinds have been devised to help control traffic. In many places today there are also special traffic police to see that the rules are followed. But in spite of our traffic rules, there are a great many accidents on our highways. Now that we have wonderful roads, we have the problem of how to make these roads safe.

ROBIN All over the United States the robin is likely to be the first bird children know by name. It lives in all parts of the country. It seems to like to be near people. It is big enough to be seen easily. And it hops about on the ground in plain view when it is hunting for food.

In the southern United States the robin can be found all the year round. Most of the robins from the northern states go south for the winter. They come back early in the spring. The sight of a robin is usually one of the first signs of spring.

This bird got its name by mistake. When the early settlers saw it, it reminded them of the robin redbreast they had known in the Old World. So they called it a robin.

But it is not a close relative of the Old World robin. It is a much closer relative of the bluebird and the thrushes. It belongs to the thrush family.

The robin builds a very sturdy nest. It is made of sticks, leaves, and grass cemented together with mud. The nest is often close to a house. It may even be on a porch. The mother robin lays from three to five beautiful blue eggs in the nest. The baby robins that hatch from them are almost naked and are very helpless. They have big appetites. Finding worms and insects for them keeps the parent birds busy. In about ten days the young robins are covered with feathers. But they do not yet look much like grown-up robins. They have speckled breasts that remind us that they are cousins of the thrushes.

Robins, like people, eat both plant and animal food. Some fruitgrowers object because robins eat some of their fruit. But robins pay for the fruit they eat by eating harmful insects. (See BIRDS.)

ROBIN HOOD There was a great archery tournament at Nottingham Town. The sheriff of Nottingham had offered an arrow of pure gold to the winner of the match. The sheriff hoped that one of those who came would be Robin Hood. For there was a reward of 200 pounds for Robin Hood and the sheriff was eager to capture him.

The most famous archers from all the surrounding country were at the match. But there was no one dressed in a suit of Lincoln green—the color that Robin Hood always wore. "He is a coward," the sheriff said to himself, "and was afraid to come."

The shooting began. At last only three men were left in the match. One was Gil o' the Red Cap, and another was Adam o' the Dell. These two men were well known to the people watching them. The third was a stranger who had a patch over one eye and wore a tattered red suit.

Each of the three shot an arrow. All three arrows were near the center, but the

According to legend Robin Hood stole from the rich.

stranger's was the closest. Then Gil o' the Red Cap shot again. His shot was so good that the crowd gasped. They were sure that he had won the prize. But up stepped the stranger. His arrow flew straight to the center of the target. No one could hope to do as well as the man in red. The sheriff gave the stranger the arrow of gold.

That night the sheriff gave a big dinner. In the middle of the dinner an arrow flew in through a window and landed on the table. On its tip there was a note. "Today you gave the prize," it said, "to Robin Hood." The stranger in the tattered red suit had been Robin Hood.

This is one of a great many stories about Robin Hood. He lived, the stories say, in Sherwood Forest more than 700 years ago. He had a merry band of men who, too, always wore suits of Lincoln green.

Robin and his men were all outlaws. They were hiding, that is, because they had broken a law of some kind. Many of them had done nothing worse than kill a deer that belonged to the king. Little John, Will Scarlet, Alan a' Dale, and Midge the Miller were four members of the band. Friar Tuck was the chaplain.

The band was loved by all the country folk. For it stole from the rich to help the poor. No poor man asked in vain for help from Robin Hood. And all the while Robin and his band of men lived a happy life in the forest and had many adventures.

Robin Hood probably was not a real person. The stories about him are probably just stories. However, they at least show what kind of person would have been a hero in England 700 years ago.

Some people believe that there really was a Robin Hood and that finally the king, Richard the Lionhearted, pardoned him and made him the Earl of Huntingdon. There is a tombstone which tells that under it lies the Earl of Huntingdon, who was once called Robin Hood. But the tombstone is not 700 years old. It may have been made by someone who wanted people to believe the Robin Hood stories. (See ARCHERY; ENGLAND'S HISTORY; MYTHS AND LEGENDS.)

ROCKEFELLER CENTER "A city within a city." This is what Rockefeller Center might be called. Its 15 buildings cover 12½ acres in the heart of New York City. In it about 34,000 people work. More than 900 firms have offices there. There are more than 20 eating places, a post office, and an 800-car garage. Radio City Music Hall in the Center is the largest indoor theater in the world. There are shops of many kinds, broadcasting studios, and big exhibition halls. The consuls of 20 foreign countries have their offices in the buildings. There are acres of roof gardens and an outdoor skating rink. More than 125,000 people visit it on an average day. The tallest building in the group is the 70-story RCA Building. The Observation Roof on the 70th floor is 850 feet above the street. It provides a wonderful view of New York.

The group of buildings gets its name because it was built by John D. Rockefeller, Jr. The first building in the group was started in July of 1931. Altogether the Center has cost more than 100 million dollars. And new buildings are added from time to time. The Time and Life Building was completed in 1959.

The buildings have straight lines and little decoration. They suit their purpose

Rockefeller Center in the Heart of New York City

very well. The builders of many earlier skyscrapers thought a great deal about making their buildings beautiful. What they did to make a building beautiful sometimes interfered with its usefulness. The buildings in Rockefeller Center follow the newer idea that usefulness comes first.

Even though usefulness has come first, much has been done to make these buildings beautiful. The straight lines themselves are pleasing. So is the pale tan stone the buildings are made of. Besides, there are murals and bronze figures and other inside decorations. The famous Prometheus Fountain is in the plaza.

The land on which Rockefeller Center is built belongs to Columbia University. In 2069 the Center will become the property of that university. (See FOUNTAINS; NEW YORK CITY; SKYSCRAPERS.)

ROCKETS In a fireworks display on the Fourth of July there are almost sure to be some skyrockets. With a loud swish a skyrocket goes into the air. High above the ground the head of the rocket bursts into bright-colored stars. The chief part of a skyrocket is a heavy paper tube, open at one end. It is filled with a powder made of charcoal and sulfur to burn and a chemical to furnish the oxygen needed for burning. When the powder starts to burn it produces hot gas that shoots out of the tube. As the gas shoots out it pushes the rocket in the opposite direction, high into the air. When the driving powder is used up, a special powder in the head of the rocket is set on fire. It produces the fireworks.

The Chinese had rockets much like our skyrockets more than 700 years ago. But these rockets were not fireworks but weapons to be fired at an enemy.

The idea of using rockets as weapons spread far and wide from China. As the centuries went by, rockets were made bigger. Metal cases took the place of the paper cases. The head was made so that it would explode when it struck anything. But for a long, long time rockets were not a great success. One line in the "Star-Spangled Banner" mentions "the rocket's red glare." Apparently the rockets the British were shooting while Francis Scott Key wrote the song did not do much besides light up the sky.

The story was quite different in World War II. In that war rockets were very important weapons. The famous V-2 rockets did enormous damage to English cities when they were fired across the English Channel by the Germans. The V-2's were huge rockets that weighed several tons.

The fuel of the V-2's was not a powder. Instead, it was alcohol. Liquid oxygen furnished the oxygen needed to make the alcohol burn. Oxygen is usually a gas. But it can be changed to a liquid by cooling it. The fuel worked so well that it sent the V-2's 70 miles above the ground and clear across the channel. They traveled a mile a second.

Although the V-2's were German weapons, the Germans did not make the first liquid-fuel rockets. The first were made by Robert Hutchings Goddard, an American. Goddard was the first great rocket scientist. It was Goddard who designed the first rocket with more than one stage, or step.

In a rocket with more than one stage, the fuel in the bottom section burns first. It sends the rocket high into the air. Then when its fuel is used up, this section drops off. The fuel in the second section now starts to burn and gives the rocket another push. If there is a third section, the second section would drop off when its fuel was gone, the fuel in the third section would start burning, and so on. There is enough fuel in each stage to last only a few seconds.

A great deal of experimenting has been done with rockets since World War II. There are several reasons for this:

Rockets are needed for weapons. Weapons far better than the V-2's have now been made. Guided missiles are being built that will land on targets hundreds or even thousands of miles away.

Rockets are needed for launching satellites. Already a number of satellites have been launched successfully.

Rockets are needed for exploring. Planes with rocket engines have gone high into the stratosphere, and unmanned rockets have told scientists a great deal about the upper air and about outer space.

Space travel, moreover, will probably depend on rockets—rockets big enough to carry passengers inside. Airplanes could never leave the earth and go traveling about in space because they can fly only in air. Because it is the air that holds them up, balloons could never go above the air. But rockets need no air to hold them up and no air to make their fuel burn.

On October 11, 1958, the United States sent up Pioneer, a rocket which set a new record. It did not go as far as it was supposed to go, for it was supposed to reach the moon. But it traveled 79,120 miles out into space—about a third of the way to the moon. Then it fell back to the earth and burned up after it entered our ocean of air.

Pioneer was called a "successful failure" because its radio sent down important messages. These messages, for example, told scientists more about a zone of deadly rays the satellites had discovered. Scientists now know that this zone is doughnut-shaped.

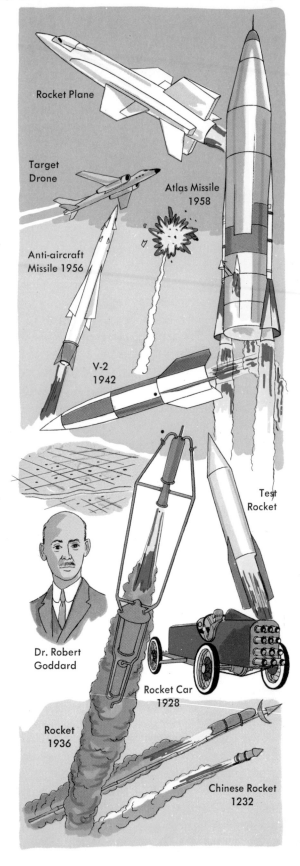

Rocket Plane

Target Drone

Atlas Missile 1958

Anti-aircraft Missile 1956

V-2 1942

Test Rocket

Dr. Robert Goddard

Rocket Car 1928

Rocket 1936

Chinese Rocket 1232

The chief reason for the failure of Pioneer was that it was not sent in quite the right direction. Because its direction was a few degrees off, it did not follow exactly the course through the air that was planned. It did not quite reach the speed it had to have to escape from the earth—a speed of 35,250 feet a second (about 7 miles a second, or 25,000 miles an hour). It got up to only 34,400 feet a second.

Aiming will always be a critical part of sending a rocket off on a journey into space. Nothing in the universe stands still. All the while the earth is traveling around the sun, the other planets are traveling around the sun, too, and the moons of the planets are traveling around the planets.

Suppose a rocket is being aimed at the moon. Then it must not be aimed at where the moon is when the rocket starts off. It must be aimed at the place where the moon will be by the time the rocket has gone far enough to reach it.

A very tiny mistake here on the surface of the earth could make a rocket miss the moon by thousands of miles. Thinking of the spokes of a wheel will help you see why this is so. Spokes that are close together near the center of the wheel are much farther apart at the rim of the wheel.

It is not at all surprising that not all the rockets sent up to explore space are a success. Pioneer I was a 4-stage rocket, 88 feet tall. It had about 300,000 separate parts. Some of its working parts were as delicate as the works of a tiny, expensive watch. All the parts must work perfectly together. And there are thousands of chances for something to go wrong.

The problems of getting a rocket ship to escape from the earth may prove to be easier than the problem of getting the ship back to earth safely. If it enters the air too fast, it will burn up just as Pioneer I did. But scientists are confident that all the problems can be solved and that space travel will in time be possible. (See SATELLITES; SPACE TRAVEL.)

ROCKS The crust of the earth is made mostly of solid rock. No matter where a person is on the earth, there is solid rock beneath him. The rock may be covered with a deep layer of soil. It may be covered with several feet or even several miles of water. But a hole dug deep enough anywhere on the earth would reach solid rock.

There are a great many kinds of rock in the earth's crust. It takes a great deal of studying to know all of them. But they can all be divided into three big groups. These three groups have rather hard names. The names are igneous rocks, sedimentary rocks, and metamorphic rocks.

"Igneous" comes from a word that means "fire." All igneous rocks are made from rock so hot that it is liquid. Some are formed from hot, liquid rock that pours out of a volcano. We call such rock *lava*. Some igneous rocks are formed from *magma*, liquid rock that is below the surface of the ground.

The first rocks formed in the earth's crust were igneous rocks. Igneous rocks are still being formed today.

The pictures on this page show four common igneous rocks. These rocks can be told from one another quite easily.

Obsidian is often called volcanic glass. It looks very much like black glass. This rock is pretty, but very few things are made of it. It breaks in a peculiar way when

IGNEOUS ROCKS

Pumice

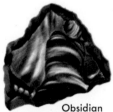
Obsidian

Basalt

Granite

polio. It left him a cripple. His legs were almost useless for the rest of his life. But many people believe that his illness helped him, too. From that time on, he seemed to understand people and their problems better. In 1928 he was elected governor of New York. Just four years later he was elected president of the United States.

Roosevelt became president when the people of the country were much discouraged. Businesses were failing and banks were closing. Roosevelt took some steps at once that gave the country hope. Very soon he started his "New Deal" program. This program was a great help to laboring people, farmers, and people without work. So many people all over the country thought of Roosevelt as their best friend that he was easily re-elected for a second term.

Roosevelt had one way of getting in touch with the people of the country that earlier presidents had not had. He could talk to them by radio. Sitting beside his fireplace he could reach millions. He had a wonderful voice for broadcasting. Many of his talks began with "My friends."

By the time Roosevelt had finished his second term, World War II was under way. The United States was not yet in the war, but the war was affecting the country a great deal. People were unwilling to change presidents at such a time. Roosevelt was elected for a third term. Soon afterward Pearl Harbor brought the United States into the war. Roosevelt steered the country through many months of that war. He had many conferences with the leaders of other countries. He was honored in many lands.

Again when it was time to elect a president Roosevelt was chosen. But he did not live to see the war end. He died in Warm Springs, Ga., on April 12, 1945.

Many lists have been made which rank the presidents. On these lists some presidents are called great, some good, and some only fair. On almost every such list Roosevelt is among those called great. (See STATESMEN; WORLD WAR II.)

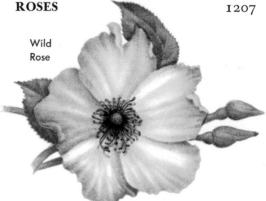

Wild Rose

ROSES A flower shop is almost sure to have roses for sale. For roses are probably the best liked of all flowers. But roses do not have to come from flower shops. We can raise them for ourselves in our yards and gardens. Farmers even plant roses of a certain kind as fences.

There are many kinds and colors of roses. Some scramble over fences and walls, others climb up trellises, and still others are bushes. The flowers may be almost any shade of red, pink, or yellow. There are pure white roses, too. Wild roses have five petals, but most of the roses we raise have many times five petals.

Rosebushes have seeds. They are formed in little fruits called rose hips. But if a rosebush seed is planted, the new plant may produce roses quite different from the rose the seed came from. Therefore, most rosebushes are raised from branches.

All roses belong to the family of plants called the rose family. It is a big family. In it there are many plants besides roses. Apples, pears, peaches, cherries, strawberries, almonds, and bridal wreath are a few of the other plants in this big family. (See FLOWER FAMILIES.)

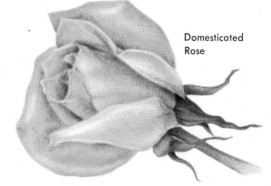

Domesticated Rose

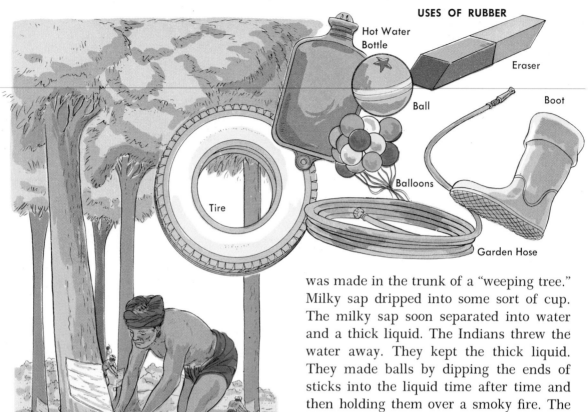

USES OF RUBBER

Hot Water Bottle

Eraser

Ball

Boot

Balloons

Tire

Garden Hose

Tapping the Rubber Tree for Latex

RUBBER When the early Spanish conquerors came to the New World, they found the Indians playing with balls that bounced. The balls were made from the milky juice of a tree the Indians called *cahuchi* (KOO chee). The word means "weeping tree."

The Spaniards did not pay much attention to the material in the balls. They were hunting for gold and other riches. Bouncing balls did not seem important.

Two hundred years later some Frenchmen exploring the lands along the great Amazon River reported that the Indians were making shoes and bowls and bottles of caoutchouc (KOO chook). This word, of course, came from the Indian name for the "weeping tree." The explorers found how the Indians got the caoutchouc. First a cut

was made in the trunk of a "weeping tree." Milky sap dripped into some sort of cup. The milky sap soon separated into water and a thick liquid. The Indians threw the water away. They kept the thick liquid. They made balls by dipping the ends of sticks into the liquid time after time and then holding them over a smoky fire. The sticky liquid became firm and dark.

When caoutchouc was taken to Europe, no one was much excited about it. Anything made of it was brittle in cold weather and sticky in hot weather. But it did get a new name. When the famous English scientist, Joseph Priestley, found it would rub out pencil marks, he called it rubber.

When rubber got its name, a half-inch cube of it sold in England for what would be about 75 cents in American money now. If rubber cost as much today, the tires for a car would sell for about $3,000.

In 1823 a Scotsman, Charles Macintosh, found that he could make good raincoats by putting a layer of rubber between two layers of cloth. His raincoats were called mackintoshes. In the same year a London coachmaker, Thomas Hancock, made the first rubber bands.

But rubber did not come into its own until Charles Goodyear, an American, made a discovery. In 1839 he found out that when sulfur was added to rubber and the mixture heated, the rubber became much easier to use. It did not become sticky or brittle. Goodyear's way of treating rubber is called vulcanization.

Many uses were now found for rubber. Ships began traveling far up the Amazon to get it. The rubber all came from "weeping trees"—really Hevea trees—in the Amazon forests. When the English found that rubber was very useful, they arranged to have seeds of the Hevea tree brought secretly from Brazil to England. They wanted to start rubber plantations in their lands in southeastern Asia. Rubber plantations were a success. By 1912 more rubber was coming from the plantations of the Far East than from Brazil. By 1932 those plantations were producing almost all the rubber for the entire world.

On a rubber plantation the milky sap from the trees is gathered by many workers. Some of it is shipped away while it is still a liquid. Some is made into sheets of rubber on the plantation. It is then packed into big bales for shipment.

The invention of the automobile stepped up the demand for rubber. In 1896 the first air-filled rubber tires were made. In that year the United States used 19,000 tons of rubber. Fifty years later the amount had jumped to more than 1,000,000 tons a year.

When World War II began, the supply of rubber from the Far East was shut off. Scientists had found that there were other plants with a milky juice that would furnish rubber. Goldenrod is one. But there was no hope of getting enough rubber from them. There was no hope of getting enough rubber from the wild trees of Brazil. Artificial rubber was the only hope. Soon several different kinds of artificial, or synthetic, rubber were being made. The chief chemical in most of today's synthetic rubber is butadiene, made from petroleum.

Rubber has many uses today. For some of these uses natural rubber is better. For some artificial rubber is better. For still others a mixture of the two is best. (See GOODYEAR, CHARLES.)

RUMANIA This country of southeastern Europe is sometimes called one of the Balkan states. The southern part of it is in the Balkan Peninsula. Its next-door Balkan neighbors are Yugoslavia and Bulgaria. Hungary borders it on the west, and the Soviet Union on the north and east. Since 1947 Rumania has been one of the countries controlled by communists behind the "iron curtain." Some changes may have been taking place there that we do not know much about.

Today the country is not quite as big as the state of Oregon. It has changed size often during its history. It has had to give up part of its land to its neighbors time after time, and at other times it has gained land from them.

For more than 200 miles, the Danube River forms the border between Rumania and its Balkan neighbors. The mouth, or rather the mouths, of this great river are in Rumania. The river has been a great help to the country. Bucharest (BOO ka rest), Rumania's capital and biggest city, is on a branch of the Danube.

The central part of Rumania is mountainous. The mountains have been a kind of fortress for the Rumanians. The people could protect themselves there whenever their country was invaded. East and west of the highlands, there are gently rolling plains in which there is much fertile soil.

Rumanian Flag
Farmer
Bucharest
Oil Well
Wheat
Vegetables
Tobacco

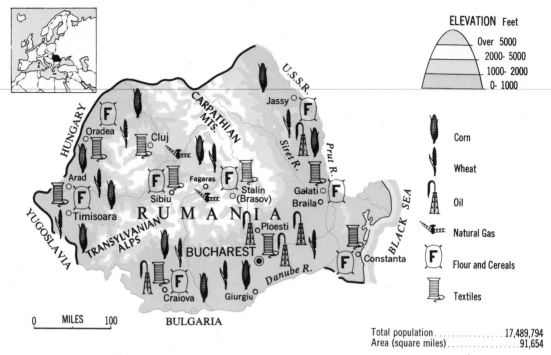

ELEVATION Feet
Over 5000
2000- 5000
1000- 2000
0- 1000

Corn
Wheat
Oil
Natural Gas
Flour and Cereals
Textiles

0   MILES   100

Total population 17,489,794
Area (square miles) 91,654

And, in most places, there is rain enough for crops. More than two-thirds of all the Rumanians are farmers. Many of the very simple homes in which they live are made of sun-dried brick.

As the map above shows, the main crops are corn and wheat. A kind of corn-meal mush is the chief food of many Rumanians. Among other crops raised are barley, rye, sugar beets, grapes, and tobacco. There are not as many cattle and sheep as we might well expect. But in recent years their number has been steadily increasing.

The map also tells that much oil and natural gas are mined in Rumania. Textiles and flour are among the important products of the factories. The government has done a great deal to make farming methods less backward than they were. New factories have been built. But many Rumanians are poor. Much of what is produced goes to the government.

Bucharest is the chief center of trade and manufacturing. Parts of the city are beautiful. They remind many people of Paris. But other parts have narrow, crowded streets with shops like those in cities in Asia. It is no wonder. For plains near the city are part of a great natural highway between Asia and central Europe. Hordes have traveled in both directions along this highway. (See BULGARIA; DANUBE RIVER; HUNGARY; YUGOSLAVIA.)

RYE The grass family furnishes us and our farm animals with more food than any other plant family. And rye is one of the important members of the family. It is not as important as two of its close relatives, rice and wheat, but it will grow in some places where wheat and rice will not grow. It can stand cold better than wheat and far better than rice.

Rye flour, from which rye bread and crackers are made, comes from the seeds, or grains, of rye. The seeds are also used in making liquors. Rye whiskey and kvass, a Russian beer, are made of rye.

The whole rye plant, grain and all, is used as food for farm animals. Rye straw, the dried stems of rye plants, can be woven into mats. And it makes good packing material for china and glassware. (See BREAD; CEREALS; GRASSES.)

S

The letter S came from this letter in the earliest alphabet: ᘰ . The Phoenicians changed its curves to straight lines (ᘻᘻ). It looked like the W of today. The Greeks turned it sidewise (Ɛ) and then changed its shape somewhat (Σ). The Romans wrote it with curves again (S) but not with the same curves it had in the beginning. It came down to us from the Romans without change.

S stands for four different sounds in English words. It has a different sound in each of these words: *easy*, *sister*, *vision*, and *sure*.

SAFETY A hundred years ago a one-year-old child in the United States had only a fifty-fifty chance of growing up. Diseases such as scarlet fever and diphtheria killed a great many children. Today there are excellent ways of fighting such diseases. A one-year-old has a very good chance of growing up if he does not have a bad accident. Accidents are today's most frequent killers, so far as children are concerned. And accidents cripple a great many children that they do not kill.

Accidents occur to children in all sorts of places—at home, on the street, at school, in public playgrounds, at places to swim, and on camping trips. There are now many more chances for accidents than there used to be. Automobiles, power tools, electric wiring, and easy ways of starting fire have brought new dangers.

A child cannot be vaccinated against accidents as he can against smallpox. No medicine will keep him from having accidents. Of course, there are ways of lessening the chances of accidents. On the streets traffic policemen help prevent accidents. At beaches and swimming pools there are lifeguards. Tools are built to be as safe as possible. Signs give warning of danger. But for the most part a child must take the responsibility for keeping himself safe from accidents. Most accidents are caused by carelessness.

Besides being careful, a child can help by following good health rules. A child who is well and strong has a better chance of avoiding accidents than one who is not.

Of course, grown people have accidents, too. A great deal has been done to make work in mills and factories safer. The same

SAFETY MEASURES

Lifeguard at the Beach

LIFE GUARD

Policewoman

SCHOOL CROSSING

Safety Patrol Boy

Steer with Both Hands

Obey Signs Warning of Danger

Put Your Toys Away

Use a Ladder to Reach High Places

Put Out a Fire Cautiously

police and guards that protect children protect grownups, too. But many grownups are careless just as many children are. Some cause accidents to themselves. Some cause accidents to others. There is an accidental death every seven minutes among the grown people of America. Clearly safety is a problem for everyone.

SAHARA The Sahara is a big desert that stretches across the northern part of Africa. The word "Sahara" means "desert" in Arabic. The Sahara is nearly as big as the whole United States.

Though the Sahara is very dry, there is a little rain. After a rain grass grows. Herders live in the desert. They keep moving from place to place to find grass for their camels and goats. The herders live in tents, which are easy to move. Such wanderers are called "nomads."

Of course, the herders must have water for themselves and their herds. They camp near places where wells have been dug to water underground.

Scattered through the Sahara there are oases, areas where there is enough water for crops. The biggest oasis is along the Nile. It is very crowded. Most of the oases are small and have only small villages in them. In the small oases wells furnish the water. Camels walk round and round the

Arab Traveler Coming on an Oasis

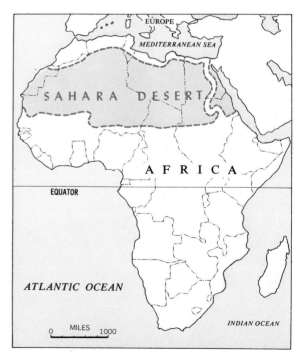

EUROPE

MEDITERRANEAN SEA

S A H A R A   D E S E R T

A F R I C A

EQUATOR

ATLANTIC OCEAN

INDIAN OCEAN

MILES
0   1000

wells turning wheels that lift up leather buckets full of water. The buckets are emptied into irrigation ditches that carry water to the fields and orchards. The chief crop is dates.

The houses in the villages are brick. Their thick walls help to keep them cool in spite of the daytime heat outside. The villagers trade with the desert nomads.

Travel in the Sahara is mostly by camel. A caravan of camels is a common sight. But buses now reach some oasis villages. Today there is new interest in the Sahara. Oil has been found there. (See DESERTS.)

ST. LAWRENCE RIVER After the voyages of Columbus explorers from many parts of Europe set out to find their fortunes in the New World. Some of the French explorers traveled deep into North America along a great river one of them named the St. Lawrence. French settlers followed and settled along the river. Even today many Canadians who live near the St. Lawrence speak French.

For more than 100 miles the St. Lawrence is now the border between Canada and the United States. It carries water from the Great Lakes to the Atlantic. Together with the Great Lakes it makes a water highway more than 2,000 miles long. The St. Lawrence would be a better highway if it were not so far north. It is frozen over for several months a year.

Until recently big ocean-going boats could go no farther west than Montreal, Canada's greatest port. Shallows, falls, and rapids beyond that point made a bottleneck. Smaller boats with the help of canals and locks were able to get through. But shipping was hindered. Now the new St. Lawrence Seaway makes every port on the river and the Great Lakes an ocean port.

The United States and Canada worked together on the Seaway. They deepened, widened, and straightened channels. They built new canals, locks, and dams.

Along with making a better highway for boats, the Seaway project furnishes electric power. And it is a wonderful example of how two nations can work together.

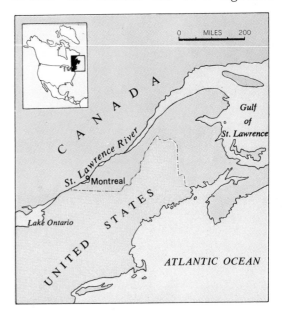

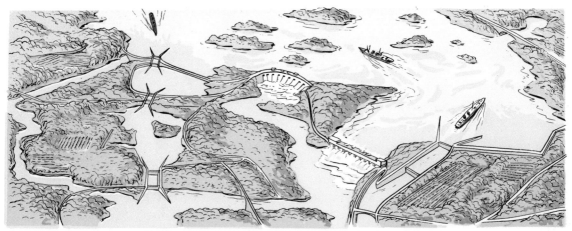

Air View of the International Section of the St. Lawrence Seaway

Silver Salmon

King Salmon

The salmon fights upstream, climbing man-made ladders around dams, to lay its eggs.

SALMON Some fishes live in the ocean all their lives. Others live their whole lives in lakes and streams. Still others spend a part of their lives in salt water and the other part in fresh water. The salmon is one of these fishes.

There are Pacific salmon and Atlantic salmon. The salmon of both oceans travel from fresh water to salt water and back. But their travels are not just the same.

Pacific salmon do most of their growing up in the sea. When the female salmon are ready to lay eggs, they come to shore and start up a river. Male salmon go with them. After the eggs are laid, the male salmon fertilize them. If the eggs are not fertilized they will not hatch.

The travels of the salmon upstream are often hard. The fish have to swim against the flow of the river. Sometimes they have to jump up falls and rapids. And the journey may be several hundred miles long. But the salmon cannot be lonesome, for thousands of salmon travel upstream at the same time.

On their trip upstream Pacific salmon do not eat anything. They live on fat stored up in their bodies. By the time they reach the place where they lay their eggs, they are tired and thin. They have lost their bright color. They start back toward the sea as soon as the eggs are laid. But most of them die on the way. They make only one trip to lay eggs, or spawn.

The baby salmon that hatch from the eggs may start down to the ocean when they are only a few weeks old. They may stay where they were hatched for more than a year. After they reach the sea, they live there till it is time for them to make the long trip upstream.

Atlantic salmon make several trips to fresh water to spawn. The baby fish stay in fresh water for two years before they first travel to the sea.

Both Pacific and Atlantic salmon come back to the river where they were hatched to lay their eggs. How they can find their home river no one knows for sure.

Salmon are among the best food fishes. There are big salmon fisheries in northwestern United States. Much of the salmon catch is canned. The Columbia River is famous for its salmon. So is Alaska. (See FISHES; FISHING; GAME FISHES.)

SALT "He is not worth his salt." "He is the salt of the earth." Both of these are common sayings. They show that salt is an important substance. It is even more important today than in the past.

At times salt has been used as money. Our word "salary" comes from *sal*, the Latin word for salt. The Roman soldiers used to be paid partly in salt.

The Arabs used to believe that eating another person's salt meant that you would do him no harm. It was a bad sign if anyone refused to eat salt when he was a guest. In some parts of Africa it is still good manners, when you meet a friend, to let him lick your cake of salt.

There are superstitions about salt, too. Spilling salt is supposed to bring bad luck. But the person who spills the salt can keep the bad luck away if he throws a little over his left shoulder. Another superstition is that you can catch a bird if you sprinkle a little salt on its tail.

Salt is something which everyone has to have. We cannot live without it. Of course, most of us like the taste of salt, too.

Sea water has salt in it. There is so much salt in the oceans that if it were all taken out and spread over the United States it would make a layer more than a mile deep. But most of the salt we buy comes from deep in the ground. It comes from layers of rock salt there. The layers were formed when salty seas of long ago evaporated. Later the salt was covered with other rocks.

It is not hard to get salt from the layers of rock salt underground. Mines can be dug down, and the salt taken out in blocks. Or water can be forced down through pipes to the salt and then pumped up again. The salt that has been dissolved in the water can easily be taken out of it.

Most of the salt we buy is in tiny crystals. Under a microscope they look like tiny cubes of glass.

We could not use salt for money now, for it is much too plentiful. We are sure that there is enough salt in the ground, to say nothing of the sea, to last millions of years.

It is good that there is so much, for we are using huge amounts of it. We use millions of tons of salt every year.

Of course we do not use all that salt to flavor our food. We use some to keep meat from spoiling. We use some in melting the ice on sidewalks. But we use most of it in making other chemicals.

Chemicals made from salt are used in the manufacture of rubber and steel and dyes and drugs. Chemicals from salt are used to soften water and to bleach cloth. They help in scouring wool and making leather. The list could go on and on. A great many of our factories of today would be forced to shut down if there were no more salt. (See COMPOUNDS; CRYSTALS; GREAT SALT LAKE; OCEANS; PETROLEUM; SUPERSTITIONS.)

Salt is often mined like coal.

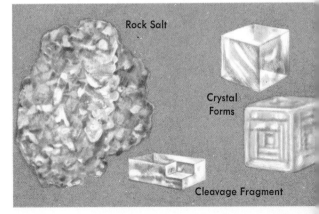

Rock Salt

Crystal Forms

Cleavage Fragment

Making a sampler helps to develop sewing skill.

SAMPLER In the early days of the United States children did not romp and play as much as they do now. For a part of every day little girls were supposed to sit quietly and sew. Samplers were one of the kinds of things they often worked on.

The picture shows a sampler. It is a piece of cloth with embroidery on it. The embroidery is the kind we now call cross-stitch. Many samplers had all the letters of the alphabet embroidered on them. Many had pictures and mottoes, too.

Children seldom work samplers now, but many samplers have been handed down to us. Most of the samplers we see today are framed and are hanging on walls like pictures. Some of them are so well done that it is hard to believe that children worked them. Many museums have collections of samplers. (See SEWING.)

SAND One of the commonest of all the substances in the world is sand. It is found on the shores of nearly all lakes and seas. There is almost nothing but sand for hundreds of miles in some of the world's great deserts. Sand is found in many other places, too. Most soil is part sand.

The wind often piles sand up into hills called dunes. A sand dune may move over farms and forests as the sand is blown up one side and over the top.

Sand is formed from rocks of many kinds. There was no sand at all when the earth was new. There had to be time for rocks to break up into tiny bits. Grains of sand are formed in the same way pebbles

are, but sand grains are smaller. Some sand is finer than other sand. But even in coarse sand the grains are tiny. There is room for thousands of them in a teaspoon.

Most grains of sand are bits of quartz. Most of them have sharp corners. Because quartz is very hard, wind carrying sand can carve rocks into strange shapes.

Sand is useful in many ways. Glass is made of sand. Concrete has sand in it. So has the mortar used in building walls of stone or brick. The big filters for filtering water are filled with sand. Sandpaper is used in every tool shop. The list of uses for sand could be made very long. (See COMPOUNDS; CONCRETE; DESERTS; DUNES; EROSION; GLASS; NATURAL BRIDGES; QUARTZ.)

Moving sand dunes have destroyed fertile farms.

SAN FRANCISCO Spread over hills on the peninsula south of the Golden Gate is the city of San Francisco. The Golden Gate is the narrow entrance from the Pacific Ocean to San Francisco Bay. No other city has such a setting as San Francisco. From the "Top of the Mark" in clear weather one gets magnificent views of the gorgeous setting and what man has built there. "The Mark" is short for the Mark Hopkins, a hotel near the heart of the city.

To the north is the long, orange bridge across the Golden Gate. It is so high that the largest ocean vessels easily go under it. To the east, crossing the Bay, is the San Francisco-Oakland bridge. This double-deck bridge is more than 8 miles long. The two bridges link the city to the East

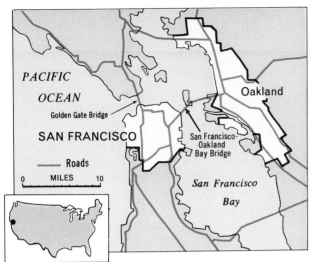

San Francisco was wrecked by an earthquake.

Bay area and to the redwood forests, farm-lands, and oil fields of California.

Skyscrapers and other fine buildings mark the business district. Streets lead down from it to the busy Bay waterfront. Here are warehouses, and docks for ships of many kinds. Other streets lead up from the business center to the homes on the upper slopes of the hills. Many streets are up very steep slopes. It is not easy to walk up these steep streets. But cars, buses, autos, and cable cars make the climb. Visitors often ride the old and noisy cable cars. They are one of the unusual things that help make San Francisco different. High on the hilltops and on the upper slopes are beautiful parks, winding drives, and lovely homes.

San Francisco is a city of about 800,000 people. It is a manufacturing and trade center. Many people from the Bay area come into San Francisco for work and for play. Its colorful past adds to the charm of the city. People from many lands came at one time or another and left their mark on the city. Spanish explorers and missionaries were among the earliest to come. The Gold Rush in 1849 brought people from almost all the countries of the world. There are many Chinese in San Francisco. Chinatown makes visitors feel as if they were in China. There is even a Chinese telephone exchange. But the Chinese young people all speak English. The fish markets

and restaurants at Fisherman's Wharf are "musts" to most tourists.

San Francisco has left behind the wild gaiety of the 1870's and the horrors of a great earthquake in 1906. It is today a thriving city with all the charm and dignity of a stately queen.

SAN MARINO Only two countries in the world are smaller than the tiny country of San Marino. They are Monaco and Vatican City. The smallest state in the United States, Rhode Island, is 30 times as big as San Marino.

This tiny country is in the Apennine Mountains that run north and south in Italy. Italy surrounds San Marino on all sides. Almost all the people of the little country are farmers.

San Marino claims to be the oldest nation in Europe. It was founded about 1,500 years ago. The rulers are elected. (See MONACO; VATICAN CITY.)

The capitol of San Marino looks like a fortress.

FIRST MAN-MADE
SATELLITES

Vanguard

Sputnik II
with Dog

Small Vanguard

Sputnik I

SATELLITES The moon is a satellite of the earth. The word "satellite" comes from a Latin word for "attendant," or "companion." The moon travels around the earth as the earth travels around the sun. Some of the planets in our solar system have several moons, or satellites.

Our moon has a definite path, or orbit. So does every other satellite. The moon is circling fast around the earth — about 2,300 miles an hour. It does not run away from the earth in spite of its speed, for the earth's gravity will not let it. But it is traveling too fast to fall to the earth.

To many people today "satellite" means "artificial moon." When scientists found that rockets could be built that would rise hundreds of miles above the earth's surface, they began to plan such a moon.

Different scientists made different plans, but they were all very much like this: A hollow ball or cylinder would be built with room for scientific instruments inside it. A multi-stage rocket would carry it high above the earth. At first the rocket would go straight up. But then it would be made to turn so that it would travel in an orbit around the earth.

To keep the earth from pulling it down at once the satellite would have to reach a speed of 18,000 miles an hour. It would have to travel faster than the real moon because it would be so much closer to the earth that the pull of gravity would be much greater. On the other hand it must not be going too fast or it would run away.

The instruments in the satellite would send down messages by radio to stations on the earth. The messages would be about such things as cosmic rays, temperature, the thinness of the atmosphere, sunlight, and meteors and meteorites.

Since the satellite would not be above the ocean of air, the air, although very thin, would gradually slow the satellite down. Finally it would fall toward the earth. As it fell through the air, it would get so hot that it would burn up.

On October 4, 1957, there was much excitement, because the Soviet Union had succeeded in sending up an artificial moon. This moon was called *Sputnik*, the Russian word for "traveling companion."

Sputnik I weighed 183 pounds. It went around the earth in a little more than 96 minutes. Its orbit was not a perfect circle. Sputnik was 156 miles above the earth's surface at its lowest point and 560 miles high at its highest point.

About a month later Sputnik II was launched. It carried the first space traveler —a little dog named Laika.

On January 31, 1958, the United States launched its first satellite. Explorer, as it was named, weighed between 30 and 31 pounds. Its orbit reached more than 1,500 miles above the earth's surface.

During the next six months the U.S.S.R. launched Sputnik III (2,925 lbs.). And the United States launched Vanguard (3¼ lbs.), Explorer III (31 lbs.), and Explorer IV (38½ lbs.). Sputnik I, Sputnik II, and Explorer III, after hundreds of trips around the earth, fell and were burned up.

From the satellites scientists have learned a great deal. They are taking it all into account in making plans for space travel. (See ROCKETS; SPACE TRAVEL.)

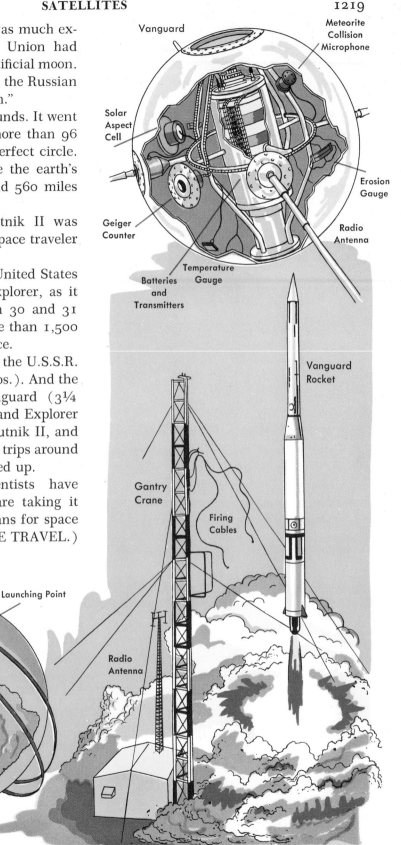

Vanguard

Meteorite Collision Microphone

Solar Aspect Cell

Geiger Counter

Erosion Gauge

Radio Antenna

Temperature Gauge

Batteries and Transmitters

Vanguard Rocket

Gantry Crane

Firing Cables

Radio Antenna

Satellite Circling Earth

Satellite

Launching Point

Orbit

Savages live by gathering food in the land about them.

SAVAGES "You are acting like savages" children are sometimes told when they are cruel or when they have bad manners. Such a saying is not fair to savages. Most savages follow carefully their own ideas of good manners. And not all savages are cruel. Savages are merely people who are not yet civilized. They live much as our ancestors lived thousands of years ago.

A glimpse of one group of savages will give a better idea of what "savage" means. Deep in the forests along the Amazon River in South America the Witoto Indians live. The tribe is made up of small clans. In each clan there are about 200 people.

Each clan has one big house. It has a frame made of logs held together with vines and covered with a thick layer of palm leaves. There are no partitions in the house, but each family has its own place and its own fire. Hammocks made of vines and slats of wood, and benches made of logs are the only furniture. The back part of the house is the home of the chief. His family may be very large because any women or children taken captive in fighting belong to him.

Cutting down trees for a house is not easy, for the Witotos have only stone axes. Their other tools are made of wood or bone. They have no metals.

The Witotos raise only a little of their food. The women gather fruits and roots from the forest. The men hunt and fish. Hunters use blowguns or traps to get wild animals for food. Sometimes the darts they use are poisoned. Fishing is done with wooden spears, bone hooks, or baskets that act as traps.

These Indians cannot read or write, but they know the ways of the forest. No civilized person could read as much from such signs as faint footprints, broken twigs, and bruised leaves as they do.

The Witotos believe in good and evil spirits. They believe, too, that some of the animals of the forest have magical powers. They are very much afraid of the jaguar and the anaconda. These particular animals are never killed for fear the clan might be harmed by their magic.

Sometimes different clans fight. But they also have feasts and dances together. Drums made of hollowed out tree trunks boom out the invitations. The drums can be heard for 20 miles.

A council helps the chief of a clan make decisions. The members even vote on important questions. They vote in a strange way. A man who has a plan explains it. Then he dips a stick into a pot of tobacco syrup. He licks the stick and passes the pot around. Everyone who agrees with him puts in a stick and licks off the tobacco.

These savages never travel far from home. They fashion a few dishes of clay and bake them in their open fires. The little clothing they wear is made of soft bark.

Not many savage tribes are as backward as the Witotos. Most of the savage tribes that are still left in the world live—like the Witotos—in isolated areas that are far from civilization. (See CANNIBALS; ETIQUETTE; SUPERSTITIONS.)

SCALES AND WEIGHING Many things are bought and sold by weight. We buy sugar by the pound, and coal by the ton, and more precious materials by the ounce or even by the grain. To weigh out a certain amount of anything or to find out how much something weighs we use scales.

The pictures show some of the many kinds of scales that have been invented. Weighing with a simple balance is easy. To weigh out a pound of candy, a pound weight is put in one pan and the candy is put in the other till the two pans balance.

Or if a buyer has picked out the candy he wants, it can be put in one pan and enough weights to balance it put in the other.

Of course, a big, loaded truck could not be weighed with a simple balance. Even if such a balance were big enough, the weights, unless a great many were used, would be too heavy to handle. On balances to weigh things that are very heavy, levers may be arranged so that a one-pound weight balances 1,000 pounds.

With some kinds of scales no weights are needed. Springs or levers inside the scales move a pointer on a dial.

Weighing is important for other things besides buying and selling. Doctors weigh their patients to find out what progress they are making. Mothers use scales to see whether their babies are gaining as they should. Travelers by plane weigh their luggage. Packages sent by mail or express are weighed. Scientists use scales to help them in their experiments.

Some scales are very sensitive. Some, for instance, can show that a piece of paper is heavier after a single word has been written on it.

Scales may do more than weigh. They may also figure prices. Suppose a butcher is selling a piece of meat at 68 cents a pound. He sets his scale at 68 cents. Then he puts the meat on the scale. The scale tells him both the weight and the price. (See WEIGHTS AND MEASURES.)

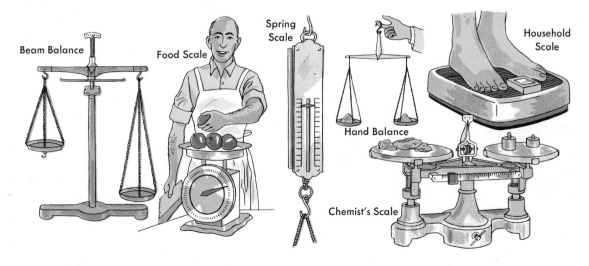

Beam Balance

Food Scale

Spring Scale

Hand Balance

Household Scale

Chemist's Scale

South American Condor (Vulture)

SCAVENGERS Nature has a clean-up brigade — living things that use as food refuse from plants and animals and dead plants and animals. The members of this brigade are called scavengers. Without them the earth would not be fit to live on.

The most numerous scavengers are tiny plants called bacteria. These and some of their fungus relatives make plant and animal materials decay as they get food from them. By causing decay they make the earth cleaner and the soil richer. Some tiny one-celled animals called protozoa are scavengers, too.

Given time enough, these tiny plant and animal scavengers could do all the scavenger work needed. But there are bigger scavengers that speed up the work.

Some scavengers keep the water of lakes and streams fit for other living things. Among these are crayfish and snails. Some of them are useful in aquariums. If a tadpole in an aquarium dies and is left in the water, bacteria finally clear it away by making it decay. But as it decays, harmful materials are formed. The water, we say, becomes polluted, and the living plants and animals there may die. But a big snail or a crayfish would make short work of the dead tadpole.

There are many insect scavengers. Water-scavenger beetles belong to the clean-up brigade. Dung beetles and blowflies do, too. Some insects even act as undertakers. The sexton beetle is one of these. It lays its eggs in a small animal and then buries the animal. When larvas hatch from the eggs, they eat the animal.

In most of the big groups of animals there are scavengers. The best scavengers of the ocean shores are the spiny-skinned animals. The starfish is one of them. Certain worms feed on dead plants and animals. Among the bird scavengers are the gulls and the vultures. The best-known mammal scavengers are the hyenas. (See BACTERIA; FUNGI; PROTOZOA.)

SCHOOLS A child in America may start to school when he is only two or three. For there are nursery schools for very young children. From nursery school he may go to kindergarten. Even if he has not gone to nursery school or kindergarten, he starts in the first grade of grade school, or elementary school, when he is about six. In most grade schools there are eight grades.

EXAMPLES OF SCAVENGERS

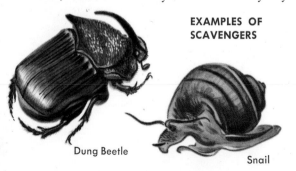

Dung Beetle

Snail

Eastern Starfish

After the eight grades of grade school come four grades of high school. The seventh and eighth grades and the first year of high school may be in a separate school called a "junior high school."

By the time he finishes high school a student has usually decided what kind of work he wants to do. Suppose a boy decides that he wants to be a chemist. After high school he goes to a college or a university for a four-year course. Perhaps his first two years of this course will be taken in a junior college.

He may be able to get work as a chemist after he finishes his four-year college course. But for many jobs in chemistry he will need more training. He gets this in the graduate school of a university. He spends perhaps three years there. By the time he is ready for the work he wishes to do he may have spent more than 20 years in going to school.

Not all Americans need as much schooling for the work they want to do. But they all need some. In fact, all the states have laws saying that children must go to school for a certain number of years.

One wonderful thing about schools in America is that most of them are free. All public schools are paid for through taxes. There are also private schools for those who wish them. Those who go to private schools have to pay tuition. Some of the private schools are church schools.

Almost all countries now have schools. They are not all alike. But in all of them children are being taught to take their part in the world.

Teaching began long before there were any schools. Early man started his long climb upward by teaching others what he had learned. A cave boy did not have to start from the beginning to work out a way of killing a mammoth. His father showed him how to chip a spearhead of flint and fasten it to a long stick. He showed him how to throw the spear. Perhaps the boy in time found out how to make

Prehistoric Man Teaching His Son

Roman School

15th Century University

Early American School

Chinese School

Modern Kindergarten

Modern Elementary School

a better spear. If so, he taught his son the better way. Thus ways of doing things were passed on from generation to generation, from father to son. So were ideas concerning the world round about.

For many thousands of years all teaching was done in the family. But after men learned to write, teaching could not all be done in this way. In ancient Egypt, for example, only a few people could write or read. Some of them made a living by reading and writing. They were called scribes. If a boy wanted to learn to read and write —perhaps he wanted to be a priest or a scribe—he had to go to a scribe to learn. Other boys who wanted to be priests or scribes might join him, and thus a school would be started.

There were schools in ancient Babylonia just as there were in Egypt. Scribes would take boys to live with them to learn to be scribes. There were schools attached to the temples, too. In ruins of ancient Babylonian temples schoolrooms have been uncovered. They have in them benches where the pupils sat. In the schoolrooms, too, copybooks have been found. These copybooks were tablets of clay with the teacher's writing on one side and the pupil's on the other. The writing was the strange "wedge" writing called cuneiform.

China, India, Greece, Rome—all these countries had schools long ago. But the schools were not for everyone. Many poor people had to go without any schooling.

In Europe during the Middle Ages most schools were church schools. The Emperor Charlemagne did much to encourage learning. He ordered the bishops to set up schools. One school was in his own palace.

Just a little later Alfred the Great, the king of England, brought in scholars from other European countries to start a school at his court. His school, like Charlemagne's, was only for boys. Girls were not supposed to need any teaching except what their mothers could give them. They were taught to cook, sew, and take care of a home.

During the later Middle Ages universities sprang up in many cities of Europe. America owes many of her ideas about colleges and universities to Europe.

In the early days of America almost all the schools were private schools. In New England there were dame schools. In a dame school a woman, often a widow, taught little boys and girls to read. For older boys there were schools taught by schoolmasters. Some of these boys would go on to college. While it was still very young, Massachusetts Bay Colony started a college — Harvard — and other colleges soon followed.

There were few free schools before the 1800's. In 1805 Governor George Clinton of New York set up a public school. From then on the idea of state-supported public schools spread fast.

The first schools in America were held in buildings built for other purposes—in homes, churches, or government buildings. There were only benches to sit on. There were no blackboards. Of course, there were no moving picture machines or basketball courts or laboratories for experimenting. The boys and girls had few books. They had no pencils, paper, scissors, or crayons. They did not even have slates. They learned from what they read and from what they were told.

Today there are fine school buildings and wonderful materials to work with. Ways of teaching, too, have changed greatly. A child, for instance, who does not learn easily is no longer put on a stool with a dunce cap on his head. Instead, the teacher gives him extra help. Courses of study have changed. Latin, which was once considered the most important subject in high school, is now studied only by the boys and girls interested in it. Courses in such subjects as art, music, science, typing, and home economics have come in in its place.

In the schools of the United States today there are about 45,000,000 students. More than 30,000,000 of them are in grade schools. Some are in special schools for deaf, blind, or crippled children, and for children who find it hard to learn. More than 8,000,000 boys and girls are in high schools. The enrollment in colleges and universities is about 3,500,000. Besides, there are business schools, music schools, art schools, and nurses' schools. It takes more than 2,000,000 people to carry on the work of schools in the United States alone. (See GOVERNMENT; INTELLIGENCE QUOTIENT; TAXES.)

University Campus

SCIENCE The word "science" comes from the Latin word meaning "to know." Science is an enormous mass of knowledge about the world around us. It includes all that has been discovered about plants and animals, earth and sky, wind and weather, what things are made of, and how things work. This great body of knowledge has been built up by watching and measuring, by keeping careful records, and by carrying on experiments.

But science is not merely a big mass of knowledge. It is a great deal more. Science is also a way of thinking—of working out answers to problems.

So much has been discovered about the world we live in that no one could possibly hope to know it all. Science, therefore, has been divided up into many separate sciences. It has, we say, many branches. The science "tree" in the picture shows some of the most important ones. But each of these branches has branches, too.

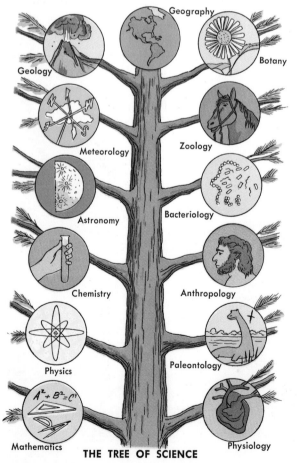

THE TREE OF SCIENCE

Some sciences are called "applied sciences." Applied sciences can be thought of as science put to work. Agriculture, for instance, is botany — the study of plants — put to work, while engineering is the science of physics put to work.

There are still many problems for scientists to solve. Some boys and girls believe that the great days of the explorers are past. Most of the world has been seen and mapped. But now space travel experts tell us that in time it will be possible to explore the moon and perhaps some of our neighbor planets. Besides, all scientists are explorers. Making some new discovery about the world right around us is as truly exploring as finding a new mountain peak or getting a view of the far side of the moon. (See ANTHROPOLOGY; ASTRONOMY; BIOLOGY; BOTANY; CHEMISTRY; EXPERIMENTS; GEOLOGY; MATHEMATICS; PHYSICS; PSYCHOLOGY.)

SCOTLAND The countries of Scotland, England, Wales, and Northern Ireland together make up a larger country. That country is the United Kingdom of Great Britain and Northern Ireland. For short it is called Britain. England, the largest country in Britain, borders Scotland on the south. Scotland is next largest.

Many men in Scotland's coastal towns are fishermen. In this mountainous country, less than a sixth of the land is fit for plowing. Summers are short, cool, and rainy. The chief farm crop is oats, and oatmeal is an important Scotch food. The custom of sprinkling salt instead of sugar on oatmeal reminds Scotch people that many of their ancestors made only a bare living. The northern highlands take up more than half of all Scotland. There we see bare peaks, narrow forested valleys, and moors purple with heather. Good pasture is scarce. But there are many pastures in the uplands near the English border.

Between the highlands and the southern uplands, a narrow belt of fertile lowland

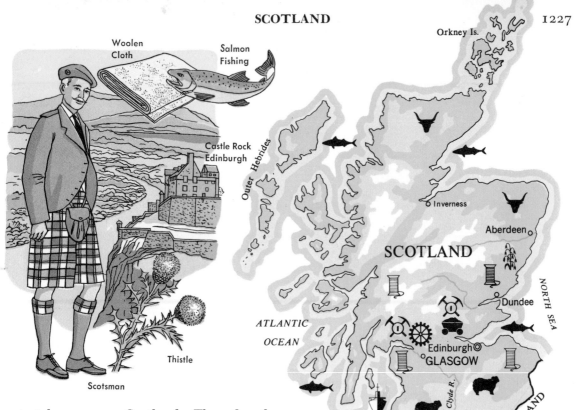

Woolen Cloth · Salmon Fishing · Castle Rock Edinburgh · Thistle · Scotsman

SCOTLAND

ATLANTIC OCEAN · Outer Hebrides · Orkney Is. · Inverness · Aberdeen · Dundee · NORTH SEA · Edinburgh · GLASGOW · Clyde R. · ENGLAND

ELEVATION
Feet
2000 — 5000
1000 — 2000
0 — 1000

Total population............ 5,145,000
Area (square miles)............ 29,795

0   MILES   100

Sheep · Iron
Beef Cattle · Fish
Coal · Oats
Shipbuilding · Textiles

stretches across Scotland. Three-fourths of Scotland's people live in this lowland—more than 1,000,000 of them in Glasgow. Coal and iron mined near this port, and wool from the uplands are used in some of Glasgow's many kinds of factories. In shipyards near by the "Queen Elizabeth" and other great ocean liners were built.

In the lowland there are many farms, too. Besides oats, Scotch farmers raise some other grains and some vegetables and small fruits. At the eastern end of the lowland is Scotland's ancient capital, Edinburgh (ED n bur o). In the "new town" part of it, there are handsome shops and homes. The city has long been a center for printing books. Famous buildings in the high "old town" part of the city are its ancient university and castle. The old castle, Holyrood, sometimes welcomes Queen Elizabeth II and her family.

Long ago, before Scotland and England were united, great families, or clans, lived in the northern highlands. Their chiefs lived in castles, but their clansmen lived in sod huts. All the Scots wore kilts of woolen plaid cloth. From time to time, they raided one another's land and also lowland farms to get enough food. Today highland pastures are still used. But hunting and fishing clubs now rent much lake and highland moor country. The highlands have become a holiday land. Today the Scots are a prosperous people. (See BAGPIPE; BRUCE, ROBERT; ENGLAND.)

STEPS IN SCULPTURING

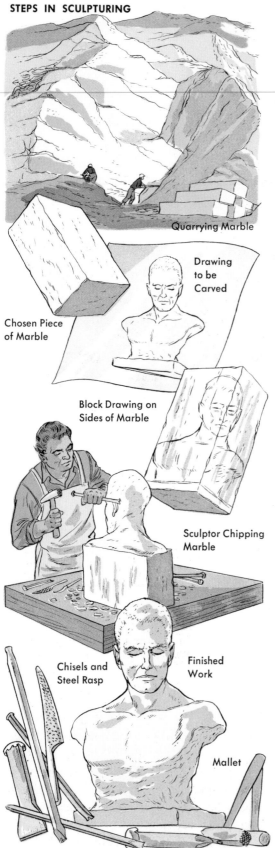

Quarrying Marble

Chosen Piece of Marble

Drawing to be Carved

Block Drawing on Sides of Marble

Sculptor Chipping Marble

Chisels and Steel Rasp

Finished Work

Mallet

SCULPTURE

SCULPTURE After a heavy snowstorm in Chicago not long ago people who passed the Art Institute saw near it a huge cat modeled in snow. The artist who made the cat was a sculptor. He had used the snow as his medium. Probably he liked the feel of the snow. A sculptor usually likes the feel of his medium whether it is marble, wood, snow, or one of the many other materials sculptors use.

The snow cat was a piece of sculpture in the round. There is another kind of sculpture called relief. In it, pictures or designs are carved on a surface and then the remaining surface is carved back so that the picture or design stands out.

Sculpture is very old. For thousands of years there has been sculpture of both kinds. Even the cave men carved the shapes of the animals they hunted on the handles of some of their tools.

Some of the statues made by the ancient Egyptians were very large. The Sphinx is one of them. It had the body of a lion to stand for strength and the head of a man to stand for intelligence. The head of this great statue is 65 feet high and 14 feet across. Some statues were portraits of pharaohs. High on a cliff above the Nile, for instance, a huge statue of Ramses II has looked down on the river for more than 3,000 years. These great statues were carved in stone. There were smaller stone statues, too. One of the most famous is the head of Queen Nefertiti. It is painted. The Egyptians also made statues in wood. In tombs many wooden figures have been found of servants going about their work. These servants were supposed to help their dead master in the afterlife.

Most of the best-known sculptures of the Babylonians, Assyrians, and Persians were relief sculptures. The scene showing Ashurbanipal hunting is carved in alabaster. Over and over again Darius of Persia had the figures of his "Ten Thousand Immortals"—soldiers who had fought in battle with him—carved in stone.

The Greeks made wonderful statues of white marble and painted them with bright colors such as red and blue. The frieze of the Parthenon is a good example of their relief sculpture. They also did much sculpture in the round. No one knows the names of the sculptors of earlier civilizations. But we do know the names of some of the Greek sculptors. Among them are Phidias, Myron, and Praxiteles.

The Romans made portraits in stone. These portraits were very lifelike.

The Gothic cathedrals of the Middle Ages had continued stories carved on their walls. People could stand in front of the cathedral and read Bible stories, not in words but in carved pictures. Many of the statues on the cathedrals are architectural; that is, they are part of the structure of the building. On Chartres Cathedral, for example, the statues are taller than real people, and serve as columns to support the arch over the main door.

In the 15th century Italy had some of the greatest sculptors the world has ever known. Among them were Leonardo da Vinci, Ghiberti, Donatello, Verrocchio, della Robbia, and, greatest of all, Michelangelo.

In more recent times many countries have given us good sculptors. Rodin of France, Thorwaldsen of Denmark, Milles of Sweden, Meštrović of Yugoslavia, and Epstein of England are a few.

Some sculptors have especially liked to design fountains. A beautiful fountain seems so alive. The sculpture in it shines with the water on it. Some sculptors are especially interested in modeling animals. Some make portrait statues just as did the Egyptians of long ago.

Suppose a sculptor has been asked to make a statue 10 or 12 feet tall. It is to be for a monument. How does he go about making such a statue?

Planning the statue is the first step. The sculptor draws a sketch of what he has in mind. A sculptor must be able to draw as well as model.

EXAMPLES OF EARLY SCULPTURE

Stone Age Sculpture on Easter Island

Assyrian Bas-relief of Ashurbanipal Hunting

Roman Bust

Ancient Greek Statue

EXAMPLES OF SCULPTURE

Pillars of the
Chartres Cathedral

"The Discus
Thrower"
Myron

Lion
Donatello

"The Madonna and Angels"   Luca Della Robbia

A sculptor needs to be able to do some things that are much like the work of a plumber. He must be able to cut lead pipe into pieces the right length and make joints like those a plumber makes. He needs a strong framework for his model in clay. But before he makes a big model he makes many little clay models. He decides which one he likes best. Then he builds a framework of lead pipe and wood and starts his big clay model. As a rule, he models the statue, but he may carve parts of it, too. He models the general shape of the biggest parts, but when it comes to the smaller details he often carves.

If his statue is to be marble or some other kind of stone he has much carving to do. He carves the stone into an exact copy of the clay model. In early times a sculptor did all the carving himself. Now he may have helpers block out the statue roughly and he may do only the fine carving to finish it. A sculptor when carving stone often wears a mask, for it is not good for one's lungs to breathe rock dust. Carving in stone is slow work. A sculptor's art takes much patience.

But perhaps the statue is to be bronze, not stone. Making a bronze statue is very different from making a marble or granite one. After the clay statue is finished, a mold is made from it. Then molten bronze is poured into the mold. As a rule statues made of bronze are more detailed than those cut from stone. The reason is plain. It is easy to pour melted metal into small places. In carving stone, a sculptor may ruin a statue in making some fine detail. He may chip off a large chunk when he wants to remove only a sliver.

Today much sculpture is abstract. A piece of sculpture may be just a form, not a representation of a person or animal or plant. This form may be meant to give a feeling of swiftness or of great joy or of ruggedness. It may be made of gold or brass or copper. Metals and wood and stone may be combined. The finished piece of sculpture may be very simple and smooth. It may be interesting because it is made of materials of different textures.

A sculptor is always interested in how his work is placed and lighted. In the case of big statues that are to be high above the ground he must have this placing in mind in making his plans. He may have to make some parts out of proportion in order to give the effect he wants to the people looking up at it. A piece of abstract sculpture is usually meant to be placed so that it has plenty of space all around it. It is often the keynote of a large room with big windows. One artist has said that a piece of sculpture should always be put on a pedestal that can be turned so that it can be seen from every direction. Poor lighting may make even a good piece of sculpture look uninteresting. If a statue is to stand out of doors where the light changes at different times of day, the sculptor must plan a statue that will look interesting in any kind of light.

Some artists say that they like to feel a piece of sculpture with their fingers before they see it with their eyes. They say that a good piece of sculpture should always make you want to feel it, not just look at it. Certainly feeling a statue may help you to get the message that the sculptor is trying to give you.

There are some very puzzling pieces of sculpture. Among them are the great stone figures scattered over Easter Island, a lonely island in the South Pacific. Each statue is carved from a single block of stone. Some of the statues are 30 feet tall and weigh many tons. Many of them have been moved miles from the quarries where they were carved and have been set up on solid stone foundations. Who carved these giant statues? What do they stand for? How were they moved? No one knows—not even the people who now live on Easter Island. (See ARTS; GREECE; MICHELANGELO; RENAISSANCE; VINCI, LEONARDO DA; WOOD CARVING.)

EXAMPLES OF MODERN SCULPTURE

"The Thinker" Rodin

"Lion of Lucerne" Thorwaldsen

"Wolf's Head" Goyri

"The American Soldier" Epstein

The seahorse can anchor itself with its tail.

SEA HORSE The sea horse is a small fish. It has gills and fins just as all fishes do. But it does not look like a fish. It swims with its head up and its tail down. Its head looks a little like a horse's head. Its tail is a little like a monkey's. The sea horse can hold itself in place by wrapping its tail around a seaweed. No other fish has this kind of tail.

The sea horse is unfishlike in still another way. The mother sea horse does not lay her eggs and then leave them as most fishes do. Instead she puts them in a pouch on the father sea horse's body. He carries them until they hatch. Then the baby fish swim away to look after themselves.

A sea horse's body is covered with small bony plates. They make a kind of outside skeleton. Many a visitor to the seashore has brought home a dried sea horse.

This little fish has been known for thousands of years. There is a picture of a seahorse on an ancient Egyptian mummy case. (See FISHES.)

SEAL Most mammals live on land. The mammals called seals all live in water. Most of them live in the sea. The ancestors of the seals were probably four-legged land animals. But seals have four flippers instead of legs. Flippers are much better than legs for swimming.

Northern fur seals are great travelers. They spend the winters roaming the ocean. In the spring they come together on the Pribilof Islands in the Bering Sea. These islands are their breeding grounds. The seals may have to swim thousands of miles to get there. The males, or bulls, reach the islands first. Each one chooses a place among the rocks for himself. Then the females, or cows, arrive to have their babies on shore. Each bull persuades as many of the cows as possible to share with him the place he chose. Every now and then, the bulls fight big battles with one another.

The baby seals are very small when they are born. But they eat a great deal and grow fast. They learn to swim by splashing about together in the shallow water near shore. After a few months they are big enough to swim out to sea. Fur seals used to be killed by the millions for their wonderful fur. Now governments protect them.

The familiar seals of circus acts are sea lions. They are close relatives of the fur seal. The harbor seal and the elephant seal are not. As the chart shows, the walrus belongs to the same large group of animals as all the seals.

Elephant seals get their name from the big nose and the great size of the male. A full-grown male may be 18 feet long and weigh thousands of pounds. The harbor seal is much smaller. It gets its name because it is so often seen on shore.

FAMILY TREE OF SEALS, SEA LIONS, AND WALRUSES

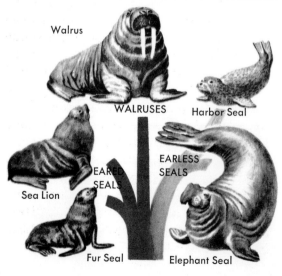

Walrus

WALRUSES

Harbor Seal

EARED SEALS

EARLESS SEALS

Sea Lion

Fur Seal

Elephant Seal

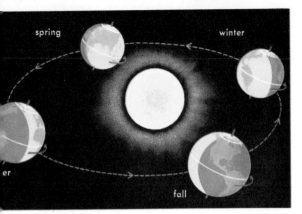

SEASONS In many parts of the world there are four seasons every year—spring, summer, fall, and winter. Summer, of course, is the time of warm weather and winter of cold weather. And fall and spring are the in-between seasons.

Many parts of the world have these four seasons. Lands near the equator, however, have pretty much the same temperature all year. Those lands that do have four seasons do not all have them at the same time. When lands north of the equator are having winter, lands south of the equator are having summer.

The traveling of the earth around the sun helps cause the seasons. But there is more to the story than that. As the earth travels, it spins on its axis, and its axis is tilted. It is always tilted in the same direction. The North Pole therefore is turned away from the sun for part of the yearly journey and toward it for part. The northern half of the earth has summer when the North Pole is turned toward the sun. It has winter when the North Pole is turned away from the sun. When the North Pole is tilted toward the sun, the South Pole tilts away from it. The seasons south of the equator, therefore, are the northern seasons turned around.

The earth is a little farther away from the sun in June than in December. Summers would be warmer and winters colder in the northern hemisphere if it were the other way around. (See DAY AND NIGHT; EARTH; TIME AND TIME TELLING.)

SECRET WRITING One of America's best-known short stories centers around an old piece of parchment which a man finds one day. Quite by accident, he discovers part of a message in invisible ink written on the parchment. When he makes all the writing visible, the message turns out to be in cipher. After a great deal of work, he decodes the message. It leads him to a rich, hidden pirate treasure.

Edgar Allan Poe wrote this story, "The Gold Bug," more than a century ago. But it is still popular. People will probably always be interested in secret writing.

Secret writing is meant to be read only by the person for whom the message is intended. Secret writing makes use of such things as invisible ink, codes, ciphers, or combinations of these.

There are many things that everyone has at hand that make good invisible inks. Lemon juice, onion juice, and even milk can be used. So can water with sugar dissolved in it. Writing done with any of these "inks" will disappear as soon as it dries. It can be made to reappear permanently by heating the paper carefully.

Most people use "code" and "cipher" to mean the same thing. But to message experts there is a difference between them.

A "code" is a list of words that stand for other words, or maybe even whole sentences. A radio patrolman, for example, may call headquarters and say, "Signal 31." This may be code for: "An armed robbery has just occurred."

"Ciphers" are systems of changing the separate letters of a message. A simple example would be EGASSEM, which is MESSAGE written backwards. Other ciphers use symbols. Still others use certain letters to stand for other letters. "X," for instance, might always be used to stand for "e." Often friends work out a cipher to use in sending messages to each other.

Secret writing has very important uses. In wartime it is used for sending highly secret military messages. (See INK.)

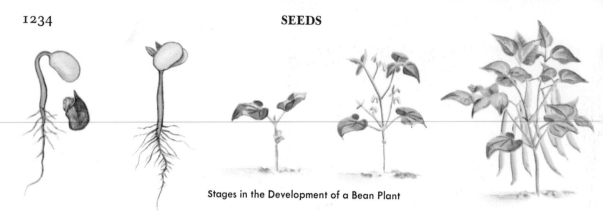

Stages in the Development of a Bean Plant

SEEDS More than half of all the kinds of plants in the world grow from seeds. Some seeds, like coconuts, are big. Some, like mustard seeds, are tiny. Seeds may be different in color and shape, too. But they are all alike in three ways. They all have a baby plant inside. They all have some food for the baby plant. And they all have a seed coat on the outside. This coat protects the baby plant and its food.

Although all seeds are alike in these three ways, they are not built on just the same plan. The pictures of the bean and the grains of corn on the next page show two plans. In the bean the baby plant is between two thick seed leaves filled with food. The baby plant and the two seed leaves fill all the room inside the coat. In a grain of corn there is only one seed leaf. Some of the food for the baby plant is stored around the seed leaf, not in it. A great many plants have seeds built on the bean plan. A great many, too, have seeds built on the corn plan.

If all a plant's seeds fell close to it, not many of them would have a chance to grow. Most seeds have ways of getting themselves scattered. Some travel by land, some by water, and some by air.

Many of the seeds that travel by air have parachutes of down. Others have wings. Most of the seeds that travel by water are light enough to float.

Some seeds that travel by land are hitchhikers. They may have sharp prickles that help them catch in the fur of animals. They may get rides in mud that sticks to the feet of birds and other animals. Birds often carry seeds hundreds of miles in the mud on their feet. Some seeds get themselves scattered by being in fruits that birds like. The birds eat the soft part of the fruit and drop the seeds.

Tumbleweeds have a quite different way of scattering their seeds. The whole plant dries up and rolls along the ground, dropping its seeds as it goes.

Witch hazel, touch-me-not, and some other plants shoot their seeds out of their seed pods. Perhaps the best "shooter" is the South American plant called the monkey's dinner bell. Some seeds coast, some crawl, and some travel about in seed holders that make good boats.

Sometimes we wish seeds did not have such good ways of getting themselves scattered. How pleasant it would be not to have to keep weeding our fields and gardens!

We eat many seeds. The food stored in seeds for the baby plants makes good food for us, too. Among the seeds we eat are beans, peas, nuts, and all the seeds we call grains. Probably the very first plants men raised were raised for their seeds. (See CEREALS; FRUITS; PLANT KINGDOM.)

Many seeds are spread by birds and other animals.

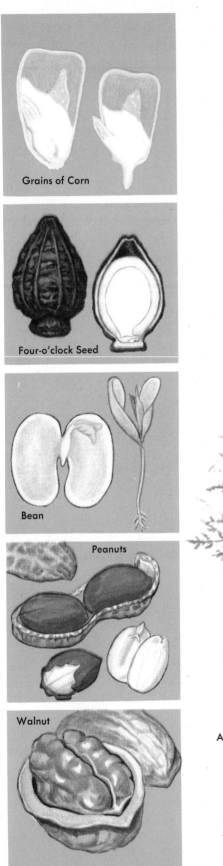

Grains of Corn

Four-o'clock Seed

Bean

Peanuts

Walnut

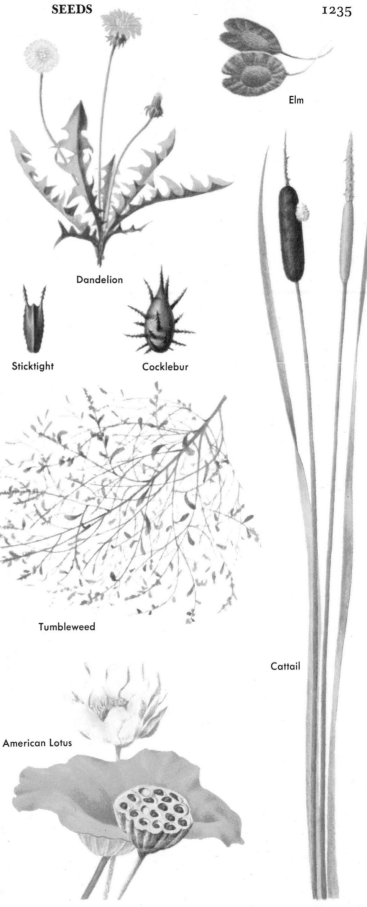

Elm

Dandelion

Sticktight

Cocklebur

Tumbleweed

Cattail

American Lotus

SEVEN WONDERS OF THE WORLD

In ancient times, long before there were great machines to help him, man showed that he was a clever builder. Some of the things built long ago were so remarkable that they are called the Seven Wonders of the Ancient World. The Seven Wonders were the Great Pyramid, the Hanging Gardens of Babylon, the Statue of Zeus at Olympia, the Temple of Diana, the Tomb of King Mausolus, the Colossus of Rhodes, and the Lighthouse of Alexandria.

First to be built of the Seven Wonders was the Great Pyramid. The pyramid was a tomb which King Khufu of Egypt had built for himself. It was made of more than 2 million huge blocks of limestone, each weighing about 3 tons. The pyramid was 481 feet high—as high as a 40-story building. Each side of the square base measured 755 feet. Many thousands of slaves worked to pull the big blocks to their proper places. After the blocks had all been set in place, the pyramid was covered with a facing of fine white limestone.

Although it was the first of the Seven Wonders to be built, the Great Pyramid is the only one of the seven still standing. A large part of the limestone facing has been removed, but the main part of the pyramid is as solid as when it was built more than 4,500 years ago. It is at Giza, not far from the present big city of Cairo.

Twenty-five hundred years ago, the city of Babylon, in the land of the Tigris and Euphrates rivers, was famous for its towering walls. The whole city was surrounded by walls. Other walls, which rose to more than 300 feet, surrounded the palace of the king. Ancient writings tell that on the tops of the walls protecting the king's palace there were gardens even more wonderful than the walls themselves. The gardens were called the Hanging Gardens of Babylon. King Nebuchadnezzar, it is said, had them planted to please his wife, who missed the trees and flowers around her former home in the mountains.

Zeus was one of the Greek gods. At Olympia in Greece the famous sculptor Phideas built a statue of him some 24 centuries ago. The statue was about 40 feet tall and was covered with thin sheets of ivory and gold. The eyes were jewels. This statue lasted for hundreds of years.

About 400 B.C. a marble temple was built at Ephesus, in Asia Minor, to the goddess Diana. The temple was remarkable for its great pillars. After standing for about 600 years it was looted and badly damaged by barbarians.

When Mausolus, the king of a part of Asia, died, a tomb was built for him at Halicarnassus in Asia Minor. This tomb was not nearly as large as the Great Pyramid, but it is supposed to have been the most beautiful tomb built in ancient times. It was more than 100 feet high. At the top there was a statue of a chariot drawn by prancing horses. Two figures in the chariot were supposedly King Mausolus and the queen. This tomb built in 353 B.C. remained standing for about 1,900 years. It was then destroyed by an earthquake, but it was so famous that the word "mausoleum" came to be a word for tomb.

In 280 B.C. the people of Rhodes, a city on an island in the Aegean Sea, had a great statue built to celebrate a victory. The statue, called the Colossus, was about 100 feet tall. It was at the entrance to the harbor at Rhodes. Some claim that the statue stood astride the harbor entrance. Others say that both feet of the statue were on the same side of the entrance. The Colossus of Rhodes was destroyed by an earthquake in 224 B.C., after it had stood only 56 years.

The Lighthouse of Alexandria in Egypt guarded a harbor, too. It was a stone tower about 400 feet high. On its top bonfires burned to warn sailors that there were rocks near by. The Lighthouse, built before 250 B.C., lasted for more than 1,500 years. (See ALEXANDRIA; BABYLONIA; GREEK MYTHS; PYRAMIDS.)

The Great Pyramid of Khufu

Temple of Diana at Ephesus

The Colossus of Rhodes

The Lighthouse at Alexandria

The Statue of Zeus at Olympia

The Mausoleum of Halicarnarssus

The Walls and Hanging Gardens of Babylon

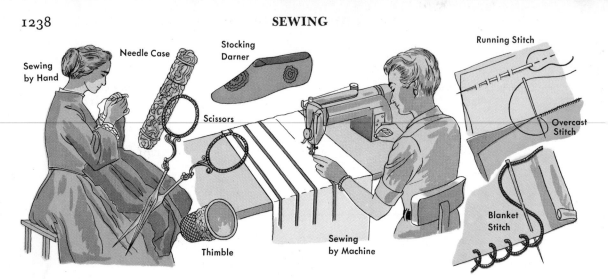

Sewing by Hand · Needle Case · Stocking Darner · Running Stitch · Scissors · Overcast Stitch · Thimble · Sewing by Machine · Blanket Stitch

SEWING Dresses, coats, suits, gloves, shoes, curtains, sheets—how hard it would be to make all such things if people had never learned to sew. Different stitches are used in making different things. But all sewing is done with needles and thread.

Sewing began so long ago that no one has any idea who invented it. Probably the very first sewing was done in the making of clothing out of animal skins.

The first needles were probably made of stone. The person sewing simply punched holes with his stone needle. Then he pushed through them the grass or thin strip of leather or whatever he was using for thread. Later, people learned to make needles of bone, bronze, ivory, and steel. They learned to put eyes in the needles. Most needles of today are made of steel. Some are big; some are small. Common sewing needles come in sizes numbered 1 to 12.

Thread is made of many different fibers and in many different sizes. Cotton, linen, silk, and nylon are a few of the fibers used. Thread, too, is numbered. No. 60 is much used in ordinary sewing. No. 40 is coarser. No. 10 is very coarse. No. 100 is fine. No. 200 is finer still.

As soon as good needles and thread could be bought, women took pride in being able to sew with small, even stitches. They did fancy sewing, too, such as cross stitching and embroidery. Even little girls learned how to "sew a fine seam."

In 1846 Elias Howe was given the first patent on a machine that could sew. Now most sewing in the United States is done by machine. Machine sewing is much faster than hand sewing. Modern sewing machines are run by electricity. With an electric sewing machine a person does not have much to do but guide the cloth and control the speed of the machine. Early sewing machines could do only straight stitching. Now the sewing machines we have can make buttonholes, tucks, and gathers. They can do pleating, darning, and sew on buttons. They can even do embroidery.

When all sewing was done by hand, most of it was done at home or in tailor or dressmaker shops. A great deal of today's sewing is done by machine in factories.

Much of the sewing still done at home is done by machine. Home sewing means also measuring, cutting, and fitting. Sewing well takes a great deal of skill.

People are not the only animals that can sew. The tailorbird sews leaves together to make a nest. The thread it uses is grass. Its bill is its needle. Tailor ants fasten leaves together with living needles. The living needles are baby ants. The grown-up ants hold the baby ants so that the baby ants, or larvas, fasten the leaves together with silk they spin. Perhaps what they do should not be called sewing. The silk sticks to the leaf edges instead of going through holes in the leaves.

SHAKESPEARE, WILLIAM (1564-1616)

England's greatest poet, William Shakespeare, was born at Stratford on Avon, a market town about 93 miles northwest of London. He was born during the reign of famous Queen Elizabeth I.

Shakespeare was earning his own living by the time he was 18. He was not yet 19 when he married Anne Hathaway. They had three children—Susanna, Judith, and Hamnet. Judith and Hamnet were twins.

Not much is known about what Shakespeare did in the years just after his marriage. Some accounts say that he taught school in the country for a while. Some say that he worked for his father, who was a glovemaker. A few years later he appeared in London as an actor and writer of plays. His plays were written in poetry.

In 1592 bubonic plague, a terrible disease, swept over London. For about two years all London theaters were closed. During that time Shakespeare began to write poems. Besides writing some long poems, he wrote more than 100 sonnets. A sonnet is a 14-line poem which has a certain regular pattern and rhyme.

When the plague was over, the playhouses were opened again. New companies of actors were formed and Shakespeare began to spend most of his time writing plays. He became a part-owner in the company for which he wrote. This company, known as the Lord Chamberlain's Men, often put on a play to entertain the royal household. Shakespeare prospered.

Shakespeare wrote some of his plays about early kings of England. *Henry V* and *Richard III* are two of these plays. They helped the English people to understand the history of their own country.

Besides his historical plays Shakespeare wrote both comedies and tragedies. *Romeo and Juliet* is one of the most famous of his tragedies. It is the story of two young lovers whose families hate each other. The play ends with the deaths of the lovers. Other tragedies include *Hamlet*, *Macbeth*, and *Othello*. Among his comedies are *A Midsummer Night's Dream*, *The Taming of the Shrew*, and *The Merchant of Venice*.

Shakespeare borrowed from other writers some of the stories for his plays. But his way of telling the stories was his own.

At the height of his success Shakespeare returned to Stratford. There he died on his 52nd birthday. He is buried in Stratford. Thousands of people visit his birthplace and grave each year.

His plays, still popular today, have been translated into many languages. Many people think that *Hamlet* is his greatest play. Even now, more than 300 years after Shakespeare died, the ambition of many actors is to be a great Hamlet. (See ELIZABETH I; ENGLISH WRITERS; RENAISSANCE; THEATER.)

Globe Theater

William Shakespeare

Stratford on Avon
Shakespeare's Home

Rehearsing *King Lear*

SHANGHAI The Chinese seaport Shanghai is a city of over seven million people. It is the largest city of China and one of the five largest cities of the world. Its name means "up from the sea." The name is a good one. Shanghai lies on mud flats 13 miles up the little Whangpoo River, which joins the mighty Yangtze River. The spot was not a very good one on which to build a city. It was hard for the people of Shanghai to get fresh water, good drainage, and firm foundations for buildings.

Shanghai, however, has a big point in its favor. It is the door to the long, broad Yangtze Valley. In the farm villages and cities of this vast area live over 200 million people. Two hundred million people furnish many customers and supply many materials for merchants and factories. These customers can be reached cheaply by steamers, oil tankers, and small river craft. Bus lines connect nearby towns with Shanghai. Railroads from most parts of China end in its stations. Shanghai has

regular air service to Peiping and other large cities of China and abroad.

One hundred years ago Shanghai was only a small fishing village enclosed by a wall. By World War II half the trade of the country passed through Shanghai. It also had nearly half of all the country's big new factories. Most of China's printing was also done in the city.

The growth of Shanghai began with the coming of British, American, and French merchants during the last century. These foreigners built up the section of the city which fronts the Whangpoo. This section has handsome boulevards lined with hotels, banks, air-conditioned department stores and movies, tall office buildings, and great warehouses near the harbor. The older Chinese section has narrow streets crowded with small shops bearing brightly painted "up and down" signs. Shanghai now has many factories and homes. There are schools and colleges for Chinese young people. Shanghai used to be a "double city." Now the foreigners have gone and all of Shanghai is a Chinese city. (See ASIA; CHINA; CITIES.)

In the port of Shanghai are small boats called sampans.

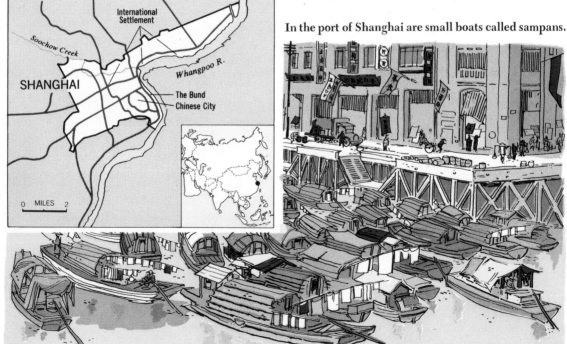

The bighorn sheep lives in the Rocky Mountains.

Sheepmen and their herds wander over the plains.

TYPES OF SHEEP

Merino

Karakul

Southdown

Dorset Horn

SHEEP Records written several thousand years ago tell about shepherds and their flocks. Sheep were tamed before people learned to write. No one knows what kind of wild sheep were first tamed. Today there are still wild sheep, but none of them is much like any of the sheep we raise. Those we raise have short legs and, as a rule, long tails. These sheep have a coat of thick wool. Their horns, if they have any, are short. They are gentle and rather stupid. Wild sheep have long legs, long coarse hair, and short tails. Most wild sheep have long horns. They are bold and quick. Man has brought about great changes in sheep since he first tamed them.

Sheep are raised for their wool, for their meat, and, in some parts of the world, for their milk and their fat. The Merino is raised chiefly for its fine wool. The Shropshire produces excellent meat as well as good wool. The Cheviot also produces good wool and meat. There are many other fine breeds.

In Asia and North Africa there are fat-tailed sheep. Sheep of this kind store fat in their tails just as a camel stores fat in its hump. A sheep's tail may weigh as much as 50 pounds. Sometimes a shepherd helps a fat-tailed sheep by giving it a little cart for its tail to rest on.

The wild sheep of today are found in mountains. One of the best known is the bighorn of the Rocky Mountains. (See ANIMAL BREEDING; DOMESTICATED ANIMALS; HOOFED ANIMALS; WOOL.)

Soft-shell clams may be dug and eaten.

SHELLFISH A great many of the animals that live in water have no backbones. A great many of these water animals without backbones do have shells or hard coverings much like shells. They are often called shellfish. The name is only half-good, for shellfish are not really fish. All true fishes have backbones.

Clams, snails that live in water, and lobsters are shellfish. Clams have two shells hinged together that can open and close. Snails have only one shell. The hard covering of a lobster is not a true shell, but the lobster is called a shellfish. There are many other shellfish.

Shellfish of a number of kinds are good to eat. Americans eat many clams, oysters, shrimps, lobsters, and scallops every year. (See CRUSTACEANS; MOLLUSKS.)

SHELLS Many kinds of animals without backbones have shells. Most of these animals live in water. They build their shells out of lime from the water. An animal's shell grows as the animal grows.

The shells of some animals are all in one piece. The shells of others are made of two parts hinged together.

Many of these one-piece shells come from snails. Snail shells are probably the shells people know best. There are water snails and land snails. All snail shells are twisted. Some of them are twisted in one direction, some in the opposite direction. Because of the way they are twisted, snail shells are called "right-handed" or "left-

handed." The left-handed whelk makes one of the left-handed shells. Most of them are right-handed.

Most of the one-piece shells in the picture are easy to pick out. It may not be easy, however, to see that the keyhole limpet, the bleeding tooth, and the abalone shells are one-piece shells, too.

Probably the biggest of the one-piece shells is the shell of the queen conch (KONGK). This shell has a beautiful pearly pink lining. When a person holds a queen conch shell to his ear he hears a roar like the roar of the sea. Many people think that they are really hearing the sea, but of course they are not. The least little sound outside will be magnified into a roar inside the big twisted shell.

Among the animals with two-piece shells are the oysters, mussels, scallops, and clams. The animals with two-piece shells are often called bivalves. This name comes from the Latin and means "two doors."

The only bivalve shells among the shells pictured are the scallop shells, the cockleshells, and the angel wing. Only one part of the angel wing and each of the scallop shells shows.

Many people collect shells for a hobby. The names they give the shells may have nothing to do with the animals that made them. Instead they tell how the shell looks. There is no way of telling from the name "angel wing," for instance, that the animal that makes this beautiful shell is really a kind of clam.

It is possible to have an interesting shell collection in a small space, for some shells are no bigger than the head of a pin. But a collection of all the kinds of shells in the world would take up an enormous amount of space. There are more than 75,000 kinds of animals with shells. Besides, the shells of some of the bivalves are even larger than the shell of the queen conch. The shell of the giant clam may be a yard across.

Shells make a good protection for the animals that have them. They are also useful to humans. Shells have been used as money in many different parts of the world. The American Indians used to use shells as money. Their shell money was called "wampum." Shells are still money in some faraway places. Many buttons and beads are made of shells. Shells are broken up and used as food for some animals. Chickens, for instance, are fed oyster shells. Ground-up shells are sometimes put on soil to keep it from getting sour.

For hundreds of millions of years animals with shells have lived in the sea. Billions of these shells have sunk to the bottom of the sea and have formed thick layers that have become solid limestone. (See BUTTONS; CAMEO; CLAMS; INVERTEBRATES; MOLLUSKS; MONEY; OYSTERS; SNAILS.)

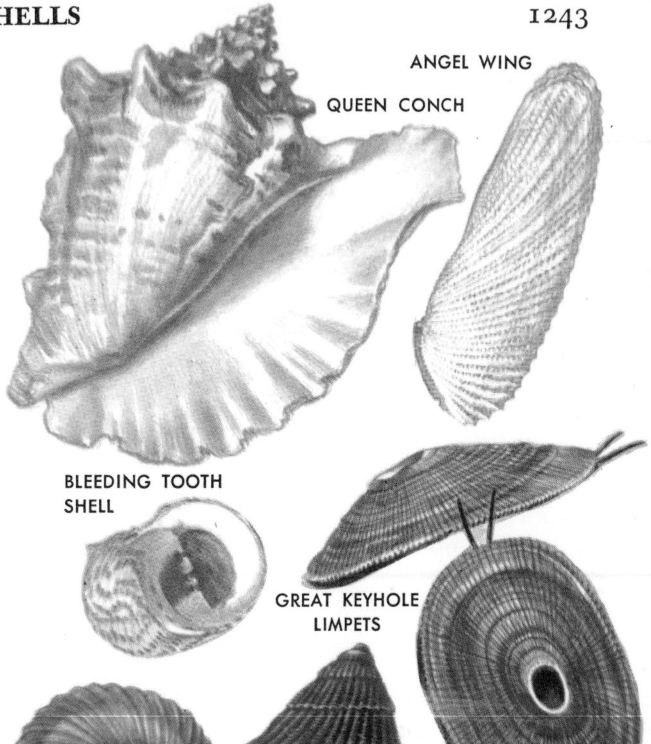

QUEEN CONCH

ANGEL WING

BLEEDING TOOTH SHELL

GREAT KEYHOLE LIMPETS

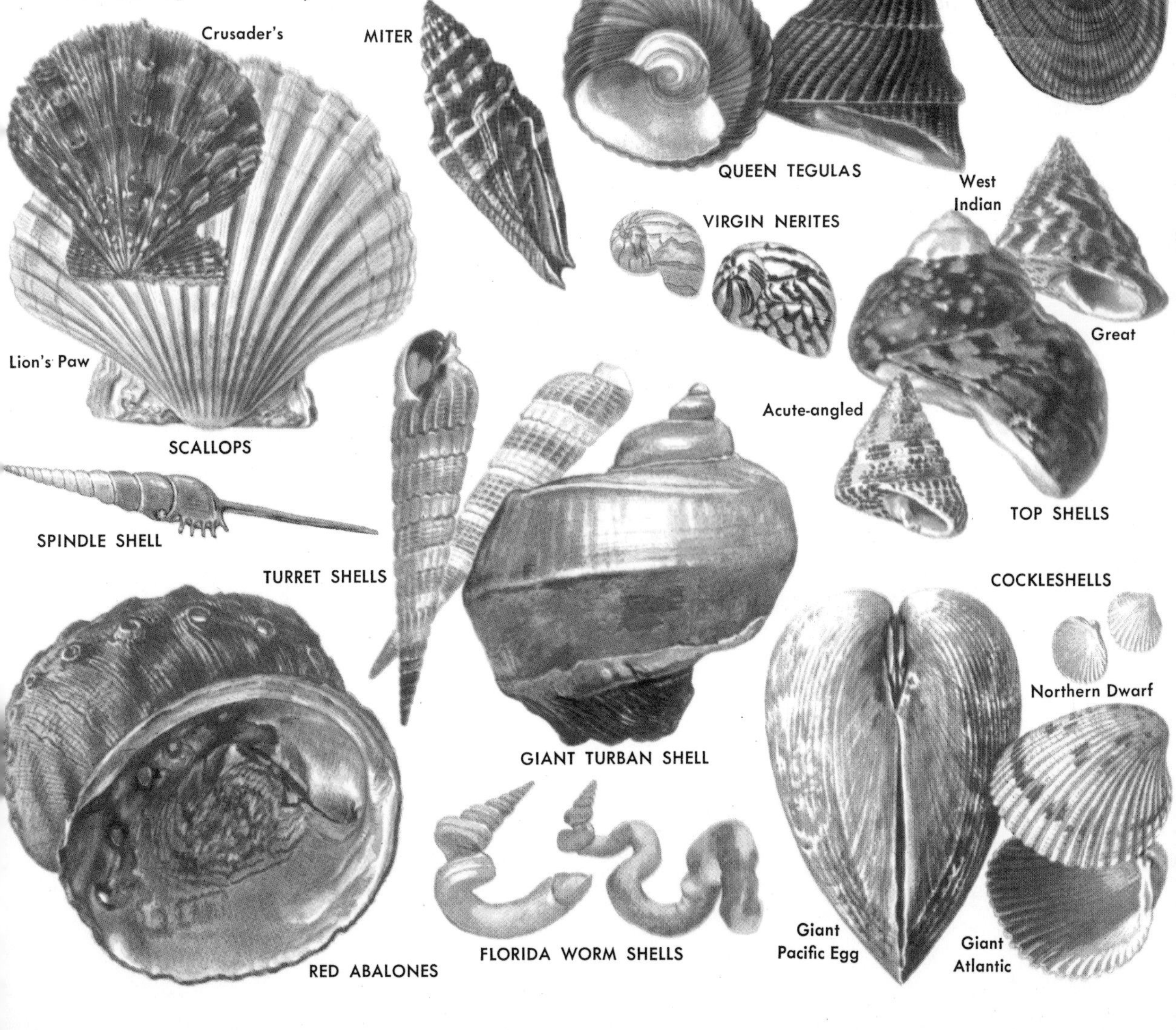

QUEEN TEGULAS

West Indian

Crusader's

MITER

VIRGIN NERITES

Great

Lion's Paw

Acute-angled

SCALLOPS

TOP SHELLS

SPINDLE SHELL

TURRET SHELLS

COCKLESHELLS

Northern Dwarf

GIANT TURBAN SHELL

Giant Pacific Egg

Giant Atlantic

RED ABALONES

FLORIDA WORM SHELLS

SHIPS All boats may be called ships and all ships may be called boats. But usually the word "boats" is saved for small vessels while "ships" is used for vessels big enough to go to sea.

A big passenger ship, or ocean liner, is a great deal like a city hotel. It has several floors called decks. On all the upper floors there are bedrooms called staterooms or cabins. Elevators carry passengers from deck to deck. Besides the bedrooms there are dining rooms, beauty shops, barber shops, stores, and lounges. Many liners have gymnasiums, a theater, a swimming pool, and a hospital. The rooms may be air conditioned. They all have electric lights. Many have telephones.

A liner is driven through the water by giant bronze propellers. These propellers are turned by steam turbines, diesel engines, or electric motors. A rudder at the back of the ship guides it. The ship is controlled from the wheelhouse, which is at the front of the very top deck. Here the captain gives his orders. Here the helmsman steers the big ship. And here is the automatic steering wheel that keeps a ship on its course out at sea.

The captain has much help in sailing his ship. Some of it comes from wonderful instruments—compasses, very accurate clocks, and weather instruments. Radio, radar, and sonar help him find out easily how far he is from shore and from other vessels and how deep the water is.

Of course, a big liner weighs thousands of tons. It can float because of the way it is built. Much of the ship is filled with air. Air is so much lighter than water that the whole boat, even with its great engines and its passengers, weighs much less than the water that would take up the same space.

The world's largest ocean liner is the "Queen Elizabeth." It is over 1,000 feet

Since early days ships have sailed the seas. For centuries sails were the most important way of moving a ship. The invention of steam power, however, brought great changes in shipbuilding.

Galley

Chinese Junk

Viking Ship

Caravel

Centerboard Sailboat

Clipper Ship

Sidewheeler

SOUTHERN BELLE

Cargo Ship

The Queen Mary, like all passenger liners, is a floating city. She provides beauty parlors, barber shops, gift shops, and game areas as well as food and sleeping accommodations for her many passengers.

The aircraft carrier "Forrestal" and its sister carriers are the largest ships in the world. Aircraft carriers carry not only enough crew to operate a large ship, but also the men and equipment necessary to maintain and launch the airplanes stored on the decks.

The Japanese surrender after World War II was signed on the battleship "Missouri." The ship also played an important part in the Korean War, but was dismantled for scrap in 1958.

long, longer than most city blocks. The world's fastest ocean liner is the "United States." It made its first trip across the Atlantic in 3 days, 10 hours, and 40 minutes. To make this fast time it sailed 35.59 nautical miles an hour. A nautical mile is a little longer than a land mile.

The pictures show a few other ships of today and yesterday. Before the days of steam engines ships were driven by oars or sails. As late as 1850 the fastest ships were sailing vessels. Clipper ships could cross the Atlantic in 12 or 13 days.

Today many of our big ships are naval vessels or cargo ships or oil tankers. The largest ships in the world are the aircraft carriers of the United States Navy. The largest cargo vessel is the "Ore Chief," an ore boat built in Japan. The largest oil tankers—there are several about the same size—were also built in Japan. These big ships all fly the flag of Liberia.

For many, many years ships were the only means of crossing oceans. Now there are airplanes. But ships can carry much bigger and heavier loads than airplanes. Ships of many kinds will keep on sailing the seven seas. (See BOATS; COMPASS; ENGINES, HEAT; GYROSCOPE; NAVY; RADAR; RADIO; SUBMARINES.)

TYPES OF SHOES

Egyptian Sandal
1450 B.C.

English Cracowe
1400

United States
Quaker 1750

American Indian
Moccasin

United States
Button 1880

Belgian
Sabot

Chinese
Lady's Shoe

Alaskan Eskimo
Muckluck

SHOES Many children think it is fun on a warm summer day to walk barefoot through grass or on bare sand. But no one thinks it is fun to walk barefoot in snow or over rough stones. It is not surprising that people learned to make shoes for themselves before they learned to keep records of what they did.

Since there is no record of the earliest shoes, we can only guess what they were made of and how they looked. Perhaps they were made of animal skin. Perhaps instead they were made of matted grass or of flat pieces of wood. Probably they were fastened on with strips of skin or with strands of grass. Most of our shoes today are made of animal skin—the tanned skin we call leather. But the upper parts of shoes may be made of cotton, nylon, plastic, silk, straw, or linen. And the soles may be made of rubber instead of leather. The heels may be made of rubber or wood.

At first shoes were only for protection. But in time they were for decoration, too. They also showed the rank of the wearer. Just for protection no one would ever have made shoes with toes so long that they had to be chained up to the knees. No one would ever have made shoes with very high heels, with toes six inches broad, or with big buckles glistening with jewels. The pictures show a very few of the many kinds of shoes that have been worn in various places at one time or another.

Today the two shoes in a pair of shoes are not alike. One is for the left foot and the other for the right foot. But having the two shoes different is not a very old idea. It goes back only about 150 years.

Of course, for a very long time all shoes were made by hand. In the beginning every family made its own shoes. But as villages grew up some people became shoemakers for other people. During the Middle Ages the shoemakers were very important members of the groups in which they lived. When the "Mayflower" made its second voyage to the New World, it brought the first shoemaker, or cobbler, to the colonies. The settlers in Plymouth were very glad to have a cobbler join the settlement.

There are still shoemakers who make fine shoes partly by hand. But most shoes are now made by machine in big factories. More than 150 different machines are used in making a pair of shoes. Many of the machines are sewing machines of one kind or another. The invention of the sewing machine was a great help to the shoemaker.

In a shoe factory a shoe goes through eight different departments, or rooms. They are the cutting room; stitching room; sole-leather room; lasting room, where the shoes are shaped to fit; bottoming room, where the outer soles are fastened on; making room, where the heels are put in place; finishing room; and packing room.

Shoemaking today is a big business. The stores of the United States sell more than 3 billion dollars' worth of shoes a year. The United States makes more shoes than any other country and ships them all over the world. (See LEATHER.)

SHRUBS Trees have woody stems. So do many other plants. Some plants with woody stems are vines. Some are bushes, or shrubs. It is easy to tell a vine from a tree; vines climb. It is not so easy to tell a shrub from a tree, especially from a young tree. Full-grown shrubs are smaller than full-grown trees and their stems are thinner. A shrub as a rule has more than one stem, a tree only one. And shrubs branch closer to the ground than do most trees.

Some shrubs are evergreen like some trees. Other shrubs drop all their leaves in the fall just as many of our trees do.

Raspberry plants are shrubs. So are the plants that bear blackberries, gooseberries, and currants. We raise many shrubs for their fruit. We often call shrubs bushes.

Rows of shrubs may be used as fences. A shrub fence is called a hedge.

A great many kinds of shrubs are raised because they are beautiful. Some have beautiful flowers. Some have bright berries. We like some for their leaves. Some can be trimmed into interesting and unusual shapes. The shrubs we raise for their beauty are called ornamental shrubs. Roses, lilacs, spirea, hydrangea, and high-bush cranberry are among the most widely planted of these ornamental shrubs. (See HERBS; TREES; VINES.)

SIAMESE TWINS In 1811 Chang and Eng, two boys, were born in Siam. Their father was Chinese. Their mother was half Chinese and half Siamese. Chang and Eng were twins, but they were not like most twins. They were joined together by a tube made of cartilage. Cartilage is the tough material which we call gristle when we find it in our meat.

The doctors said that Chang and Eng could not be separated. At least one of them would be sure to die if they were. So they remained joined all their lives. They lived to be 63 years old! P. T. Barnum, the circus man, brought them to the United States so that people could see them.

Every once in a while twins are born that are joined together. Chang and Eng were so famous that now all babies joined together are called Siamese twins. It is possible to separate some of them. There are Siamese twins among cats and dogs and other animals, too. (See BARNUM, P. T.)

SIGNALING Many ways have been worked out of sending messages with signals. Some signals are so common that people do not think of them as important message bringers. Factory whistles are a good example. Traffic lights are another.

Factory whistles are one of a great number of ways of signaling with sound. Doorbells, fire sirens, foghorns, and horns on automobiles are a few of the others. A lost hunter fires three shots into the air as a call for help. In a football game the referee blows a whistle to announce that a play is over. The natives of Africa send messages with "talking drums." Sound is a fast traveler, but it does not travel well for long distances. Messages are sometimes sent for many miles with drums, but they must be repeated along the way.

Light was used as a signal long before there were any red and green traffic lights. The fall of Troy, it is told, was announced to the Greeks at home by bonfires. The approach of the great Spanish Armada was announced to the English many centuries later in the same way. Lanterns gave Paul Revere the message that started him on his famous ride.

The ancient Greeks sent messages by arranging flaming torches in racks. There was a different arrangement of torches for each letter. When Napoleon was fighting in sunny Egypt, his officers flashed messages to one another with mirrors. A mirror used in flashing a message is called a heliograph. "Heliograph" comes from the Greek words for "sun" and "write." Hundreds of years before Napoleon's time the Persians "wrote with sunlight." They used their polished shields as mirrors. At sea today messages are often sent from ship to ship with blinker lights.

Smoke from fires can be used in signaling. The Indians were experts in this way of sending messages.

The U.S. Weather Bureau uses flags as weather signals. And ships send messages by using flags. An international flag code lets ships "talk" to one another even though the crews of the ships speak different languages. Wigwagging is a way of spelling out messages with flags.

Semaphores are much used along railroads as signals to trains. The position of the arm tells whether the track ahead is clear. Just before electricity was first used as a messenger, semaphores were used to send messages long distances. Semaphore stations were set up every few miles. An operator spelled out a message by arranging the arms of his semaphore in different positions. Through spyglasses the operator at the next station read the message and then sent it on its way.

Fog once interfered with an important message sent by semaphore. The English under Wellington were fighting with the French under Napoleon. This message came through to the English at home: "Wellington defeated." Fog had shut off the last two words: "the French." What a difference the two words made!

Sometimes signals are used even when people are close enough to talk easily to each other. Signals keep the message secret. In a baseball game, for instance, the catcher tells the pitcher with a signal what kind of ball to pitch.

The telephone, telegraph, and radio take the place now of many older ways of signaling. But they will never entirely replace the older ways. (See RADIO; TELEGRAPH; TELEPHONE.)

Foghorn

Emergency Smoke Flare

RAILROAD CROSSING

Traffic Light

Crossing Signal

Flags

STOP ON RED SIGNAL

African Signal Drum

Fire Alarm Call Box

THE GOLDEN BOOK ENCYCLOPEDIA
CONTAINS THE FOLLOWING VOLUMES

CONTRIBUTING ARTISTS

Dot and Sy Barlowe • Cornelius De Witt • E. Joseph Dreany • Bruno Frost
James Gordon Irving • Beth and Joe Krush • Harry Lazarus • Andre LeBlanc
H. Charles McBarron • Denny McMains • Harry McNaught
Ray Perlman • John Polgreen • Evelyn Urbanowich

Pauline Batchelder Adams • George Avison • Barry Bart • Ernie Barth • Charles Bellow
Eric Bender • Juanita Bennett • Merrit Berger • Robert D. Bezucha • William Bolin
Thelma Bowie • Matilda Breuer • S. Syd Brown • Peter Buchard • Louise Fulton Bush
Jim Caraway • Nino Carbe • Sam Citron • Gordon Clifton • Mel Crawford • Robert Doremus
Harry Daugherty • Rachel Taft Dixon • Olive Earle • Sydney F. Fletcher • F. Beaumont Fox
Rudolf Freund • Tibor Gergely • Douglas Gorsline • Hamilton Greene • Gerald Gregg
Marjorie Hartwell • Hans H. Helweg • Janice Holland • W. Ben Hunt
Arch and Miriam Hurford • Harper Johnson • Norman Jonsson • Matthew Kalmenoff
Janet Robson Kennedy • Paul Kinnear • Olga Kucera • Walter Kumme • John Leone
Kenneth E. Lowman • John Alan Maxwell • Jean McCammack • Shane Miller • Stina Nagel
Elizabeth Newhall • Gregory Orloff • Raymond Pease • Alice and Martin Provensen
Jerry Robinson • Feodor Rojankovsky • Roki • Mary Royt • Arnold W. Ryan
Arthur Sanford • Sam Savitts • William Sayles • Al Schmidt • Edwin Schmidt
Frederick E. Seyfarth • Robert Sherman • George Solonewitsch • Lionel Stern
Norton Stewart • Valerie Swenson • Gustaf Tenggren • William Thompson • Felix Traugott
Eileen Fox Vaughn • Herschel Wartik • Robert Weisman • Garth Williams

MAPS BY

Vincent Kotschar   Jean Paul Tremblay
Carol Vinall   Frederic Lorenzen
Rudolf von Siegl   Francis Barkoczy

COVER ARTISTS

Ned Seidler • Ken Davies • Don Moss